Salad*ish*

Salad*ish*

A Crunch*ier*, Grain*ier*, Herb*ier*, Heart*ier*, Tast*ier* Way with Vegetables

ILENE ROSEN

WITH DONNA GELB

PHOTOGRAPHS BY JOSEPH DE LEO
ILLUSTRATIONS BY EMMA DIBBEN

ARTISAN | NEW YORK

For my mother, and for the memory of my father.
For Isabel and for Hannah.

Copyright © 2018 by Ilene Rosen
Photographs copyright © 2018 by Joseph De Leo
Illustrations copyright © 2018 by Emma Dibben

Library of Congress Cataloging-in-Publication Data

Names: Rosen, Ilene, author.
Title: Saladish : a crunchier, grainier, herbier, heartier, tastier way with vegetables / Ilene Rosen with Donna Gelb.
Description: New York, NY : Artisan, a division of Workman Publishing Co., Inc., 2018. | Includes index.
Identifiers: LCCN 2017036051 | ISBN 9781579656959 (hardback with dust jacket)
Subjects: LCSH: Salads. | Salad greens. | Salad vegetables. | LCGFT: Cookbooks.
Classification: LCC TX807 .R7845 2018 | DDC 641.83--dc23
LC record available at https://lccn.loc.gov/2017036051

Art direction by Michelle Ishay-Cohen
Jacket photographs by Joseph De Leo
Case illustrations by Emma Dibben
Design by Erica Heitman-Ford

Artisan books are available at special discounts when purchased in bulk for premiums and sales promotions as well as for fund-raising or educational use. Special editions or book excerpts also can be created to specification. For details, contact the Special Sales Director at the address below, or send an e-mail to specialmarkets@workman.com.

Published by Artisan
A division of Workman Publishing Co., Inc.
225 Varick Street
New York, NY 10014-4381
artisanbooks.com

Artisan is a registered trademark of Workman Publishing Co., Inc.

Published simultaneously in Canada by Thomas Allen & Son, Limited

Printed in China
First printing, March 2018

10 9 8 7 6 5 4 3 2 1

Contents

Tiny Tomatoes, Vivid &
Surprising Style
(page 68)

Introduction

All the food I really love to make and eat is salad*ish*. The base might be leafy greens or nutty farro. The salad may be fluffy or crisp, spicy or sweet, tangy or creamy—some of my favorites are a combination of all these (and more!). Healthy, satisfying, and simple to prepare, salads can be made from anything and everything—and a salad makes a meal. Two salads are even better. Three or more is a party!

I've always been a champion eater. My first foray into cooking was at age nine, when my friends and I would attempt to outweird each other with concoctions that I, nonetheless, found delicious. What began as after-school entertainment developed into a fearlessness when it came to experimenting with flavors, and a willingness to step outside the boundaries of what people typically think go together—traits that have served me well in my adulthood. (No doubt the "Horse and Pig" sandwich on page 103 owes its parentage to my middle-school cravings.)

In my thirties, a passion for produce and cooking seasonally—sparked by the mind-blowing bounty of the nearby Union Square Greenmarket in New York City—compelled me to move my interior design career to the back burner and enroll in culinary school. Diploma in hand, I knocked on the door of the only place I wanted to work: the City Bakery. My favorite neighborhood spot, its stark interior was the backdrop for simple, unembellished pastries that resonated with my designer's love of minimalism, color, and form. This was a special place, like none I'd ever seen before. I asked for a job and stayed for fifteen years.

It was an amazing opportunity. I was given free rein in the kitchen, expanding the menu of savory dishes and purchasing everything I could from the nearby greenmarket. And the bakery grew along with me; in its tenth year, we moved to a much larger location. The delicious pastries took center stage on the dark stone counters up front while my territory grew to forty linear feet of "salad bar": counters arrayed with self-service-style platters and bowls that brimmed with an ever-changing selection of lunch items.

Everything could be made ahead and left to sit in the fridge, and it would still be delicious. It was a practical style of cooking and eating that stuck with me and became my MO as I raised my twin daughters. The recipes were adapted over time, and my favorites appear in this book—made all the more accessible by the ever-increasing availability of fresh, seasonal ingredients in farmers' markets and supermarkets nationwide.

I was living in lower Manhattan during this time, and I regularly explored Chinatown's overflowing markets, buying a few new-to-me items on each trip. There were so many exciting discoveries—from bushels of bunched greens to heaps of gnarly vegetables, plus mysterious condiments and products with incomprehensible (to me) labels—it made my head spin. I was also in striking distance of the strip of international grocers on Lexington Avenue around 28th Street known as Curry Hill for its wealth of aromatic Indian and Middle Eastern ingredients.

Combining these far-flung flavors in salads of seasonal produce and hearty grains and beans became a signature of my casual, unconventional style. I tossed Chinese black rice with fresh pea greens, and flavored them with a makrut lime dressing (see page 30). I roasted cubes of sweet potato and folded in chickpeas and Indian snack mix (see page 141). To my surprise and delight, the salad bar at City Bakery developed a cult following, with a huge crowd eager to share in all the vegetable goodness each day.

In 2013, along with kindred spirit Sara Dima, I opened R&D Foods, a specialty food shop in Brooklyn, New York. It's a tiny place with lots of ideas and a big sense of community. Every morning I make cake doughnuts, and all day long my team and I turn out brined roast chickens, sandwiches to order, and ever-rotating bowls full of salad*ish* creations, many of which you'll find in the pages of this book.

I hope you'll enjoy these dishes, that they'll encourage you to rethink your pantry and broaden your repertoire. Although the recipes are arranged seasonally, many span several seasons, and some can be made all year long. Don't be afraid to substitute one green or grain for another, and please don't stop there! Use these recipes as a point of departure for your own creative journeys. Hang out at your local farmers' market, poke around an ethnic grocery, grab an unfamiliar ingredient, and make something salad*ish*!

Japanese Eggplant
Boats, Flecked
Style (page 76)

The Salad*ish* Manifesto

Whether composing a basic leafy salad or something more complex, my guidelines come down to the following.

Start with the Best

Get the highest-quality ingredients you can find, and the freshest produce at the height of its season when possible. If you choose your ingredients carefully, you can let each one shine.

Play with Contrasting Textures . . .

For a salad that grabs your attention at first bite and draws you in, include at least one component from several of the following categories.

- **Toothsome:** Roasted vegetables, grains

- **Fluffy:** Tender lettuces, herbs, soft leaves

- **Crunchy:** Sturdy greens and their stems, nuts and seeds

- **Crisp:** Sliced or diced raw vegetables, pickled things

- **Hefty:** Potatoes, bread cubes, meat, fish, tofu, cheese

. . . and Contrasting Flavors

The best salads have components that work well together yet sing out individually. Compose your dish with some (or all!) of these elements.

- **Richness:** This can come from the oil in your dressing, from roasted vegetables, from cheese, and/or from nuts and seeds.

- **Sharpness:** The acidity of citrus juice or vinegar in a dressing accentuates flavors and brightens a dish. But before composing your dressing, consider all your ingredients—tomatoes, for instance, are acidic to begin with.

- **Sweetness:** This can be a little honey in the dressing, bits of fruit (dried or fresh), or a sweet pickled something.

- **Saltiness:** Olives, capers, bacon, and cheese offer what you're after. You'll generally want to salt the salad before you introduce these salty components, but hold back a bit if you are using shredded or grated cheese (the salt in the cheese will flavor the whole salad).

- **Spiciness:** Whether used alone or in combination, the distinct flavors of "warm" spices like cumin, cinnamon, ginger, and coriander, as well as fresh, dried, and smoked chile peppers (which add fruitiness in addition to heat), bring another layer of flavor to a dish.

Basil Dressing
(page 89)

Kimchi Dressing
(page 182)

Seeded Yogurt Dip
(page 158)

Walnut Dressing
(page 116)

Lemon-Honey Dressing
(page 120)

Experiment with Dressing

A good dressing combines acid (like lemon juice or vinegar) with a smooth, rich vehicle (like oil or mayonnaise) to balance the sharpness and help to coat the vegetables. My basic proportions are 1 part acid to 3 parts oil, but this can change depending on the sharpness of the vinegar, the ingredients I am dressing, and even my mood.

This book contains a whole library of dressings for you to draw upon. Mix and match them with any combination of vegetables or grains that appeals to you, or use them as dips, sandwich condiments, and marinades.

Pay Attention to Seasoning

This cannot be overstated. Use care and take your time—taste, taste, and taste again for the right amount of salt and freshly ground black pepper. Balance is key: sweetness against salt, richness with acidity.

Add an Element of Surprise

Sometimes it's the presence of something completely unexpected—a spoonful of kimchi, a sprinkle of nigella seeds, the addition of an unusual leaf like shiso—that makes a salad exceptional. Don't be afraid to take a chance and trust your intuition: make the dish your own.

If It Still Needs a Little Something . . .

After all the adding, tweaking, adjusting, seasoning, tasting, and seasoning again, if you find yourself saying, "This salad is missing something," the answer is often an easy one: sliced or diced red onion usually does the trick.

Shichimi togarashi

Bhel mix

Yuzu kosho

Harissa

Pickled Mustard
Seeds (page 88)

Fennel
pollen

Goji berries

Dried shrimp

Gem Lettuces, Avocado, and Tomatillo with
Buttermilk Dressing (page 107)

How to Assemble a Salad (or Something Salad*ish*)

When You Mix It

Before adding the dressing, combine all the prepped vegetables and/or grains in a bowl, toss them together, and season them with salt and pepper. Mixing everything together dry helps you avoid overhandling and bruising your ingredients, and is especially important if you will be using a thick dressing. When combining sturdy ingredients and delicate leaves, it is best to not mix the delicate ones in at all. Instead, layer them in as you arrange the salad in its serving bowl or on its platter. This will prevent the greens from wilting or flattening from the weight of the dressing and the other ingredients.

Note: Some ingredients, like red beets and black olives, shed their color, so add these items only after other components of your salad have cooled.

When You Dress It

Once the seasoning is just about right, add the dressing and gently toss the salad again, then check the seasoning one more time. Hands are my favorite mixing tool at this stage, fingers spread apart to form giant forks. Mix from the bottom up, always using two hands, lifting the food—never push down on it. Rotate the bowl to distribute everything evenly.

When You Serve It

When choosing a bowl or platter for your salad, keep all the ingredients in mind: Rimmed platters keep round items such as cherry tomatoes from rolling off the sides. Wide, shallow bowls have the most surface area to show off all the ingredients for tossed salads. Slaws and salads with more liquid are easier to scoop up when served in narrower, deeper bowls.

When you transfer your salad to a serving bowl, keep it looking natural—let the ingredients fall where they may. A bit of each one should be visible. Sometimes a few key pieces will need to be repositioned on top to make the salad look its best while still maintaining a "this just happened" look. If using small items like nuts, seeds, or herb sprigs, always reserve some to top the finished dish.

The Salad*ish* Pantry

Many of the ingredients called for in these recipes are readily available in any supermarket; getting to know the international shelves is time well spent. Other items might require a visit to an Asian grocer or specialty store, fun to do in person but just a few clicks away online if you are pressed for time. See page 199 for more sourcing information.

Vinegars

Vinegars differ in style and taste, but all have in common the bright acidity that sharpens flavors.

Cider vinegar, made from apples, is great for salads and pickling. I like Bragg brand, which was originally considered a health tonic and is now available in most supermarkets.

White wine vinegar, like the wine it is made from, tends to be less assertive, gentle enough for delicate greens.

Red wine vinegars, including varietal vinegars like **merlot** and **cabernet,** add character and can stand up to sturdy bitter greens or vegetables like green beans.

Sherry vinegar, made from the fortified wine, has a deep, almost nutty flavor and often a hint of sweetness, depending on the sherry.

Flavored vinegars can effortlessly enhance simple salads with the taste of, for instance, tarragon or shallots. A few drops of **walnut vinegar** (available in specialty stores or online) can transform a mixed vegetable or bread salad.

Rice vinegar, commonly used in Asian cuisine, is the clear choice for dressing Asian ingredients. Don't confuse it with mirin, a Japanese rice wine that is like sake but sweeter. **Seasoned rice vinegar** is both sweeter and saltier than plain, useful when you want just a hint of sweetness. Some brands contain additives—look for ones that don't. Eden is a reliable brand, and so is Marukan; both are easy to find in larger supermarkets or specialty stores.

Oils

Oils are the backbone of most dressings, adding body and richness. All oils keep longer if they are refrigerated; if they solidify, just bring them to room temperature before using. Nut oils in particular go rancid quickly if kept in a cupboard.

Have a good basic brand of **extra-virgin olive oil,** such as Whole Foods Everyday 365, on hand for using in salad dressings, for roasting vegetables, and for sautéing (contrary to popular belief, there is no reason not to sauté in extra-virgin olive oil). Use one with a bit more character or fruitiness for drizzling on finished dishes—Iliada, a great artisanal Greek brand, is easy to find and not overpriced.

Flavorless vegetable oil is indispensable when you want no added flavor at all from the oil. Choose sunflower, safflower, grape seed, or canola.

Flavored oils like walnut, pumpkin seed, or toasted sesame oil add distinct personality to a dish. A little goes a long way.

Chile Sauces, Seasonings, and Condiments

Gone are the days when "hot sauce" meant Tabasco. Now there are dozens of chile sauces to choose from, and new options pop up every day. They differ widely in chile flavor, fruitiness, and heat level, but most can be stored indefinitely in the refrigerator, so you can keep several on hand to experiment with.

Gochu, Korean for "chile pepper," is a staple in Korean cooking, and **gochujang,** a paste of chiles, fermented soybeans, and rice, is available in most supermarkets, either refrigerated in tubs near the tofu or in jars on the shelf. A spoonful stirred into a simmering broth or stir-fry opens a world of savory depth and heat at the same time. Try mixing it into mayonnaise as a spread for a pulled-pork sandwich, or as a filling for Korean-inspired deviled eggs. Mother-in-Law's brand is my go-to. **Gochugaru,** fine, seed-free flakes of dried chiles, are good for sprinkling over many dishes.

Harissa, the North African chile paste, also contains bell peppers or other vegetables and warm spices like cumin and coriander. Different brands vary in potency. Tunisian Dea, which comes in a colorful yellow tube, is high on the heat scale and pungent with coriander and caraway. Mina, which is Moroccan, also comes in milder versions. New domestically produced brands, such as New York Shuk, are well worth trying when you see them.

Chipotles en adobo are smoked dried jalapeño peppers packed in a dark, tangy tomato puree. The small cans available in the Mexican section of most supermarkets go a long way, and leftover chiles, transferred to a small container, keep for weeks in the fridge. You can use the chiles and sauce separately or whir them together in the blender—a spoonful of pureed chiles and sauce stirred into the dressing for a salad of beans or black-eyed peas instantly turns it both smoky and zesty.

Sambal oelek is Indonesian in origin. The best brands contain only crushed dried red chiles, vinegar, and salt, with no additives. It delivers a bright, powerful kick to rice and noodle dishes and salads. Look for it in jars next to the Sriracha at your grocer or Asian market.

Togarashi is the Japanese word for chiles. **Shichimi togarashi** is an aromatic seven-ingredient blend of ground dried togarashi and other seasonings, including sesame seeds, ginger, hemp, seaweed, sansho (a Japanese pepper berry), and dried citrus peel. **Nanami togarashi** is blended with more citrus peel. Pure ground togarashi is often called **ichimi togarashi.** All usually come in cellophane-wrapped small jars, found in the Asian section of the supermarket or in specialty stores alongside their frequent partners, packaged ramen and soba. Try sprinkling the dried peppers or blends on roasted vegetables or grilled meats for an unusual spike of heat.

Yuzu kosho, a spicy red or green paste made from the zest and juice of yuzu (an aromatic citrus fruit that looks like bumpy grapefruit), chiles, and salt, is another unsung condiment from Japan. Stir it into broth or use as a rub for meat or chicken to add a citrusy kick.

Southeast Asian fish sauce is the pungent powerhouse behind Thai and Vietnamese cooking. Intensely flavored, a few drops add salty depth to stir-fried dishes and dipping sauces. Look for Red Boat 40, made from whole black anchovies (not extract), available at specialty stores and online.

Grains, Beans, Etc.

Whatever the season, this corner of your pantry is the secret to whipping up a tasty and substantial meal out of practically nothing.

Barley, the ordinary pearled kind, cooks quickly, and though the "pearling" or polishing removes most of the bran, it is still considered healthier than other refined grains because the fiber is present throughout the whole kernel. Nutty-tasting and chewy in texture, it can be lightly toasted in the pot over a medium flame (stir constantly) before the water is added for an even deeper flavor. For additional health benefits, choose whole grain "hulled" barley (you'll have to cook it longer).

Black rice, which actually turns purple when cooked, is increasingly easy to find in numerous varieties from China and Southeast Asia. Some are glutinous and sticky, others are not, but they are all delicious and high in antioxidants. I like Black Cargo Rice from Thailand, but you can also use Chinese Forbidden Rice or Lundberg Black Japonica.

Bulgur is whole-grain wheat that has been cracked and partially cooked—a gift if you are pressed for time. Most people know it from tabouleh, but don't hesitate to improvise and add it to other dishes. I prefer it cracked coarse or medium for firmer texture.

Pearl couscous, a small, dried pasta that looks like a grain, is called "pearl" because of its rounded shape, and also goes by the name Israeli couscous. It has a less pronounced flavor than a grain, but that subtlety can be an advantage when you want to emphasize more delicate flavors in a dish. See the note on page 25 for instructions on toasting.

Soba is the Japanese word for buckwheat, and you'll find soba noodles in the Asian department of many supermarkets. They come in three forms: 100 percent buckwheat, blended buckwheat and wheat flour, and cha soba (buckwheat and green tea blend). All are delicious, but look for the all-buckwheat version if you are sensitive to gluten.

Farro is an ancient strain of wheat popularized in Italy, and emmer is the variety you'll usually find in the United States. It's sold whole grain, semi-pearled, or pearled—the whole grain needs a soak as well as a longer cooking time. All have a rich, nutty flavor and a satisfying toothsome bite.

Quinoa, which is supernutritious, high in protein and fiber, and gluten-free, is actually a seed in the amaranth family. It needs a rinse before cooking to remove its slightly bitter natural coating, but once that's done, it's a snap to cook. It comes in several colors (white, red, and black), any of which can stand in for another.

Hominy, made from dried corn processed with alkali, can be bought whole, cracked, or ground into grits. We call for the cracked kind, soaked and boiled, on page 89; canned hominy makes a reasonable stand-in.

Black-eyed peas, a type of dried legume cultivated worldwide and much loved in the southern United States, have a fresh, grassy quality. No soaking is necessary, and they cook quickly compared to other beans and legumes.

Chickpeas, also known by their Spanish name, garbanzos, are another handy, protein-packed legume to keep on your shelf. Rich, earthy-tasting, and meaty in texture, they have the added advantage of canning exceptionally well.

Cranberry beans, also called Roman beans or borlotti, have pretty red markings that fade when cooked and are prized for their creamy texture and full flavor. They are usually sold dried, but sometimes you can find them fresh in their pods at farmers' markets or Italian grocers. If you do, grab them and shell them—they'll be even more delicious and take less time to cook.

Lentils come dried in brown, green, yellow, red, and black. I usually choose the sturdy small green ones, also called French or de Puy, for a salad since they hold their shape particularly well. Tiny, black beluga lentils are fun, too—just make sure not to overcook them.

The Salad*ish* Tool Kit

You don't need any unusual equipment to make the recipes in this book. Listed below are the tools called for most frequently.

Colander, Spider, and Fine-Mesh Strainers

A colander is essential for draining vegetables and other ingredients. A spider, with a long handle and a wide, flattened wire mesh basket, is helpful for lifting blanched vegetables out of the pot when you are going on to blanch others in the same water. A large fine-mesh strainer is a must for quinoa, which would flow right through the holes in a colander. A tiny fine-mesh strainer is invaluable for straining the seeds out of citrus juice or the garlic out of infused oil.

Microplane

This simple, inexpensive rasp grater, all but unknown a decade ago, is now an I-can't-live-without-it item. You need a fine-bladed classic zester/grater for lemons, nutmeg, garlic, and ginger and a coarser-bladed paddle grater for cheese.

Mandoline

A supersharp slicer for vegetables, a mandoline makes quick work of ultrathin cuts. The classic French metal behemoth was once feared by many home cooks, but now safe, lightweight plastic versions are readily available for pros and non-pros alike. I particularly recommend the Japanese Benriner and the inexpensive and well-designed Oxo models, which can be washed in the top rack of a dishwasher.

Food Processor and/or Blender

Both a food processor and blender are useful for pureeing and for high-speed whipping of creamy, emulsified dressings. They can be used interchangeably in the recipes that follow. Consider also purchasing a mini version of either one, which will be useful for mixing small quantities.

Mortar and Pestle and/or Spice Grinder

I use a 3-inch-wide mortar and pestle for crushing small amounts of freshly toasted whole spices. For large quantities, a dedicated coffee grinder does the job.

Y-Shaped Vegetable Peeler

Good for more than just peeling, these peelers are also useful for shaving long thin slices of vegetables and cheese (see Quick Cut, page 85).

Sheet Pans

The pans called for in this book are the standard rimmed kind that measure 13 by 18 inches (aka half-sheets by professional cooks) and fit in most home ovens. There are quarter sheet pans, too, for smaller tasks. Have a number of each on hand. You'll be surprised at how often you use them, not only for roasting and baking but also for prepping and organizing.

Stainless Steel Mixing Bowls

Get these bowls in a range of sizes: 2-cup, 1-quart, 2-quart, 3-quart, and 4-quart. Having a few extras in the smaller sizes on hand for prep duty will make your measuring and mixing easier and help you stay organized.

Kitchen Scale

A scale with the "tare" feature, such as the one made by Oxo, lets you weigh items minus the weight of the container. It's handy to know that you can keep adding ingredients to a single bowl, "taring" the scale after each addition and measuring as you go.

Latex Gloves

Your own hands are your best tools for tossing. There's really no other way to get dressing into every bit of a grain or vegetable, so keep a box of latex or vinyl gloves around for all your mixing needs. Wear a double layer of gloves as a buffer when handling hot things.

Young & Tender

SPRING

Allegedly, the human eye sees more shades of green than of any other color—and finally, they are all back! Now is the time to celebrate with delicate buds, new flowering greens, sprouting allium bulbs, and every herb within arm's reach.

—

Couscous and Spring Allium Mix

—

SERVES 6 TO 8

2 to 4 spring onions, depending on size

2 baby leeks, rinsed

4 scallions

Kosher salt

2 cups pearl couscous

2 tablespoons extra-virgin olive oil

1 or 2 stalks green garlic (depending on size and potency), chopped

Freshly ground black pepper

1 cup Watercress Dressing (recipe follows), plus more as needed

2 handfuls of frisée, torn into bite-size pieces, or other young greens, such as baby spinach

½ cup raw cashews, toasted and roughly chopped

My favorite members of the onion family get together here, all at their spring best. Long stalks of green garlic are one of the earliest arrivals at the farmers' market. Chop the bulbs and the peeled, tender parts of the stalk for a very fresh-tasting burst of garlic flavor.

1. Trim the spring onions, leeks, and scallions and separate the white parts from the tender greens. Discard any tough outer green leaves. Chop the white parts, and thinly slice the tender green parts on the diagonal. Reserve the white and green parts separately.

2. Bring a large pot of salted water to a boil. Meanwhile, pour the couscous into a dry 9- or 10-inch skillet set over medium heat and toast, stirring often, for about 6 minutes, until light golden brown. Remove from the heat.

3. Tip the couscous into the boiling water (set the skillet aside) and cook for about 8 minutes, until tender but not mushy. Drain in a colander and spread out on a sheet pan to cool completely, then transfer to a wide bowl.

4. Heat the olive oil in the skillet over medium heat and sauté the chopped white parts of the spring onions, leeks, and scallions and the green garlic, stirring, for several minutes, until softened but still slightly crisp; do not allow to brown. Remove from the heat and stir into the cooled couscous. Season to taste with salt and pepper. Let cool.

Continued

NOW YOU KNOW

Toasting Pearl Couscous

A quick toast in a dry skillet (or on a sheet pan in a moderate oven) before boiling deepens the flavor and the color of the couscous and helps the grains maintain a firmer texture when dressed.

5. Just before serving, add half of the dressing to the couscous and toss. Add the frisée and sliced spring onion, leek, and scallion greens and toss again, adding more dressing if needed (the couscous soaks it up as it stands). Add the cashews and toss again, adjust the seasoning with salt and pepper, and serve.

WATERCRESS DRESSING

—

MAKES ABOUT 1½ CUPS

1 bunch of watercress

1 tablespoon Dijon mustard

2 tablespoons white wine vinegar

¾ cup flavorless vegetable oil

Kosher salt and freshly ground black pepper

Cut the lower stems off the watercress. Rinse and dry the leafy tops and remove and discard any thicker stems. Put in the bowl of a food processor or in a blender and pulse until finely chopped, scraping down the sides as needed. Add the mustard and vinegar and pulse to combine. With the motor running, drizzle in the oil, processing until the dressing is smooth. Season to taste with salt and pepper. Leftover dressing can be used as a dip for crudités. It will keep for several days in the refrigerator.

Snap Peas and Other Things Spring

—

SERVES 4

Kosher salt

1¼ pounds snap peas, trimmed, any strings removed

1 large bunch of chives, with flowers if available

4 tablespoons fruity extra-virgin olive oil

½ cup fresh mint leaves, very thinly sliced (see Quick Cut below)

A small handful of pea flowers, if available

A classic case of what grows together, goes together. Here the fresh herbs bring out the essence of the snap peas.

1. Bring a large pot of salted water to a rolling boil; ready a large bowl of ice water. Add the snap peas to the boiling water and blanch until bright green but still very crisp. Drain them quickly in a colander and immediately plunge them into the ice water to stop the cooking. When they are cool, drain again, blot thoroughly dry, and transfer to a serving bowl.

2. Cut all chives without blossoms into 1-inch lengths. Set the blossoming chives aside.

3. Toss the snap peas with the olive oil and salt to taste. Gently fold in the chive stems and mint and scatter pea flowers over the top, if using. Twist the reserved chive blossoms off the stems to release the petals over all. Discard the stems. Serve.

QUICK CUT

Lazy (Wo)man's Chiffonade

To thinly slice mint leaves (or other delicate herbs) without bruising and darkening them:

1 Gently scrunch the leaves together into a ball with one hand.

2 Release them a bit at a time for one quick pass with a very sharp knife.

Black Rice with Pea Greens

—

SERVES 8

Makrut Lime Dressing

¼ ounce fresh makrut lime leaves

1 cup flavorless vegetable oil

¼ cup seasoned rice vinegar

2 tablespoons Dijon mustard

Kosher salt and freshly ground black pepper

Kosher salt

2 cups black rice

6 ounces snow peas and/or sugar snap peas, trimmed, any strings removed

¼ cup shelled peas

A handful of pea greens (about 1¼ ounces), trimmed if long, or leafy Asian greens, such as tatsoi

1 lime, cut into wedges, for garnish

A feast for your eyes and your taste buds in equal measure. Makrut lime leaves are worth hunting down in Asian markets or online for their unique floral citrus flavor. But if your search proves futile, substitute the Lime Dressing on page 38 for the dressing here.

1. Make the makrut lime oil for the dressing: Lay the lime leaves out on a cutting board, whack them with the back of a heavy knife, and roughly chop them. Put them in a small saucepan, cover them with the oil, and bring just to a boil over medium heat. Reduce the heat and simmer very gently for 3 minutes, then turn off the heat and let the oil steep for 30 minutes.

2. Make the dressing: Strain the infused oil and discard the leaves. Put the vinegar and mustard in the bowl of a food processor or in a blender and pulse to combine. With the motor running, drizzle in the oil, processing until the mixture is emulsified. Season to taste with salt and pepper. Set aside.

3. Bring a large pot of salted water to a boil over high heat. Add the rice and boil until just tender, about 30 minutes. Drain in a colander and spread out on a sheet pan to cool.

4. Meanwhile, bring another pot of water to a rolling boil and ready a large bowl of ice water. Add the snow peas and shelled peas to the boiling water and as soon as they turn bright green, drain them in a colander and plunge into the ice water until cool. Drain again and pat them dry.

5. Transfer the rice to a serving bowl. Add the peas, pea greens, and half of the dressing. Toss well to combine and season to taste with salt. Add more dressing as needed (the rice soaks it up as it stands) and toss again. Fluff the rice with a fork and serve with the lime wedges on the side.

"Peas and Carrots" on Papadum

—

SERVES 4

2 large carrots, peeled

Flavorless vegetable oil for frying

4 large papadums

3 handfuls (about 4 ounces) pea greens, torn into pieces if very large

¼ cup Coriander Dressing (recipe follows)

1 teaspoon nigella seeds (also known as kalonji; see Note, page 126)

The Indian flatbread papadum, typically a vehicle for chutney, becomes airy and crisp when fried. Here papadums serve as edible "plates" for a light salad. You can also snack on them as they are, or break them up and scatter them over almost any salad.

1. Shave the carrots lengthwise paper-thin on a mandoline, turning each carrot as necessary once you get to the dense core; discard the cores or save for stock. Put the carrots in a small bowl of ice water until ready to curl and crisp them (see Note, page 137).

2. Line a sheet pan with paper towels for draining. Heat about an inch of oil in a large deep skillet over medium-high heat until it is hot enough to sizzle a broken piece of papadum. Fry the papadums one at a time for several seconds on each side, until they puff up and become lightly colored; adjust the heat as necessary—they should sizzle but not burn. As each is done, hold it for a few seconds over the skillet to drain off most of the oil, then transfer it to the paper towels. Place the drained papadums on individual serving plates.

3. Drain the carrots, pat them dry, and put in a medium bowl. Add the pea greens and 2 tablespoons of the dressing and toss well. Arrange the salad on top of the papadums. Sprinkle with the nigella seeds, drizzle with the remaining 2 tablespoons dressing, and serve.

CORIANDER DRESSING

—

MAKES ABOUT 1 CUP

1 tablespoon coriander seeds, toasted and ground

¼ cup cider vinegar

1 tablespoon honey

1¼ teaspoons Dijon mustard

¾ cup flavorless vegetable oil

Combine the coriander, vinegar, honey, and mustard in the bowl of a food processor or in a blender and pulse to combine. With the motor running, stream in the oil, processing until the mixture is emulsified. The dressing can be stored tightly covered in the refrigerator for up to 5 days. This is a good excuse to make Red (page 113) as you'll have just enough dressing left over!

Baby Carrots with Carrot-Top Pesto

—

SERVES 4

2 bunches of baby carrots, scrubbed, tops attached

2 to 3 tablespoons flavorless vegetable oil

Kosher salt and freshly ground black pepper

Carrot-Top Pesto

About 2 cups loosely packed green carrot tops (stems discarded), from carrots above

¼ cup sunflower seeds, toasted

1 small garlic clove

1½ teaspoons Dijon mustard

1½ tablespoons white wine vinegar or fresh lemon juice

1½ teaspoons honey

½ cup plus 2 tablespoons flavorless vegetable oil

Kosher salt and freshly ground black pepper

Fruity olive oil for thinning the pesto

3 tablespoons queso fresco, crumbled

2 tablespoons canned or jarred pickled jalapeños, minced

Carrots are having a renaissance, appearing at farmers' markets in a range of sizes and multicolored bouquets. I can't believe I used to throw away the tops—they are absolutely delicious when ground into a pesto.

1. Preheat the oven to 400°F.

2. Trim the carrots, leaving ½ inch of the green tops attached. Reserve about 2 cups of the remaining frilly tops for the pesto, plus several of the nicest-looking tops for garnish. Cut any fatter carrots lengthwise in half so they are all about the same thickness and place on a sheet pan. Toss with enough oil to coat, spread them out on the pan, and season with salt and pepper. Roast the carrots for 18 to 25 minutes (depending on the size), turning occasionally, until nicely browned and tender.

3. Meanwhile, make the pesto: Put the carrot tops, 3 tablespoons of the sunflower seeds, and the garlic in the bowl of a food processor or in a blender and grind to a paste. Add the mustard, vinegar, and honey and blend thoroughly. With the motor running, slowly drizzle in the oil and process until the pesto is thick but still retains some texture. Season to taste with salt and pepper. (You'll have some pesto left over; store it tightly covered in the refrigerator, and use it within the next day or two, while the color is still bright.)

4. Arrange the carrots on a serving dish. Thin the pesto with olive oil until it can be drizzled. Spoon some pesto lightly over the carrots, and transfer the remaining pesto to a small serving bowl. Top the carrots with the cheese, followed by the jalapeños, and finally the remaining 1 tablespoon sunflower seeds. Serve the remaining pesto on the side.

MORE USES FOR CARROT-TOP PESTO

• As a spread for crostini with anchovies, Pickled Carrots (page 190), and sliced radishes

• As a dressing for a wedge salad of iceberg or romaine hearts, with crumbled blue cheese, spiralized or grated carrots, and (optional) crumbled crisp bacon

• As a garnish swirled into warm or chilled carrot soup

Every-Leafy-Green-You-Can-Find Salad

—

Orange Marmalade Dressing

2 teaspoons classic Seville orange marmalade

1 tablespoon fresh lemon juice

3 tablespoons extra-virgin olive oil

Kosher salt and freshly ground black pepper

1 small head of oak leaf lettuce or other tender head lettuce, such as Boston (about 3 ounces), separated into leaves, washed, and dried

2 ounces mixed young leafy greens (see headnote)

¼ cup fresh chives snipped into ½-inch lengths

¼ cup loosely packed fresh small dill sprigs

Frilly gold and ruby-streaked mustard greens, arugula, mizuna, pea greens, purslane, baby kale, tatsoi—any and all will be delicious with this orange marmalade dressing. Young leaves with flowers attached add extra texture and elegance.

1. Make the dressing: Whisk together the marmalade, lemon juice, and olive oil in a small bowl. Season to taste with salt and pepper.

2. Toss the lettuce leaves and mixed greens together with the chives and dill in a salad bowl. Just before serving, add the dressing to the greens and toss.

Rice Noodles with Lots of Asian Herbs

—

SERVES 6 TO 8

Kosher salt

1 pound wide rice noodles

Lime Dressing (recipe follows)

1 cup baby bok choy, leaves left whole, stems sliced

1 cup fresh Thai basil leaves

1 cup fresh mint leaves

A handful of fresh garlic chives or regular chives, cut into ¼-inch lengths

1 small red onion, sliced very thin

2 small carrots, peeled and cut lengthwise into long julienne strips on a mandoline

2 tablespoons fresh lime juice

Freshly ground black pepper

Herbs on herbs on herbs.

1. Bring a large pot of salted water to a boil over high heat. Add the rice noodles and boil, stirring occasionally to keep them from sticking, for about 5 minutes, until they are just cooked through. Drain in a colander and run under cold running water to cool them quickly (make sure the noodles are completely cooled so the herbs won't wilt and darken). Drain thoroughly and transfer to a large serving bowl.

2. Toss the noodles with ¼ cup of the dressing to keep them from sticking to each other, then season to taste with salt. Add the bok choy, basil and mint leaves, chives, red onion, and carrots and toss well to combine. Add the remaining ¾ cup dressing and the lime juice and toss again. Season to taste with salt and pepper and serve.

LIME DRESSING

—

MAKES A LITTLE
OVER 1 CUP

¼ cup Sweet Lime Vinegar (page 92)

2 tablespoons Dijon mustard

¾ cup flavorless vegetable oil

1½ tablespoons water

Whisk together the lime vinegar and mustard in a small bowl. Whisking constantly, add the oil in a slow, steady stream until the mixture emulsifies, then whisk in the water to lighten it. The dressing can be stored tightly covered in the refrigerator for up to 5 days.

Semi-Scorched Chive Buds with Smoked Tofu

—

SERVES 4

1 tablespoon tamari,
or to taste

1 tablespoon mirin,
or to taste

1 tablespoon flavorless
vegetable oil, plus more if
needed

1 pound garlic chive buds,
ends trimmed, cut into
2-inch lengths

2 cups (about 7 ounces)
mung bean sprouts,
rinsed and dried

4 ounces smoked tofu,
shaved on a mandoline

I promise you, this beguiling combination of garlic chive buds and smoked tofu is worth a trip to Chinatown! Grab an extra bunch of buds for the table.

1. Mix the tamari and mirin together in a small bowl.

2. Coat the bottom of a large skillet or wok with 1 tablespoon oil. Set it over fairly high heat and add about a third of the chive buds in an uncrowded layer. Allow them to sit untouched in the pan for 2 to 3 minutes, then flip them and cook for about 2 more minutes, until they are browned in parts but still mostly green and crunchy. Using a slotted spatula, transfer them to a sheet pan to cool. Repeat with the remaining chives in 2 batches, adding more oil if necessary.

3. Transfer all the chive buds to a bowl and toss with the tamari-mirin mixture and bean sprouts. Add the tofu and toss again, taking care not to break up the tofu, then add additional tamari and/or mirin if desired and serve.

MEET THE INGREDIENT

Garlic Chive Buds

These garlic chives, budding but not yet in bloom, change flavor dramatically as they cook, going from sharp and raw oniony to sweet and mellow. Taste them as you go so you catch them at the moment of transformation.

Silky Tofu Skin with Preserved Cabbage Dressing

—

SERVES 6

One 6-ounce package of dried tofu skin

Preserved Cabbage Dressing

½ cup Tianjin (Chinese preserved cabbage)

2 tablespoons rice vinegar

1 tablespoon Dijon mustard

1 tablespoon honey

1½ teaspoons mirin

½ cup flavorless vegetable oil

¼ cup water

4 ounces mustard greens or other sturdy leafy greens, preferably Asian

4 large eggs

1½ teaspoons flavorless vegetable oil

1 cup fresh or frozen shelled edamame, defrosted if frozen

Tossed with greens, beans, and scrambled eggs, pasta-like tofu skin is my comfort food from another mother. Tianjin is a type of Chinese preserved cabbage, sold in Chinese markets. If you can't find it, substitute Kimchi Dressing (page 182) using white kimchi for the Preserved Cabbage Dressing here. It is tangier but just as garlicky.

1. Put the tofu skin in a large bowl and cover with 2 quarts hot water—it will soften immediately. Stir with a wooden spoon; it will break apart into large pieces. Transfer to a colander set over a wide bowl to drain off the liquid for about 20 minutes, occasionally pressing down on it gently with a rubber spatula. Blot thoroughly dry.

2. Make the dressing: Rinse the preserved cabbage in a bowl of cold water, breaking it up with your fingers. Drain it in a colander, pressing down to squeeze out the excess liquid, and repeat with fresh water. Drain and squeeze it dry.

3. Put the preserved cabbage in the bowl of a food processor or in a blender, add the rice vinegar, mustard, honey, and mirin, and pulse to combine. With the motor running, drizzle in the oil and then the water, processing until the dressing is thick and creamy.

4. Trim the stem ends off the mustard greens. Slice the leaves crosswise into 1-inch-wide ribbons and slice the stems about ¼ inch thick. Set aside ½ cup of the stems; save the extra stems, dice, and pickle for another use (see Note, page 114).

5. Beat the eggs with a fork in a small bowl. Heat the oil in a medium skillet over medium heat. Add the eggs and scramble them. Cool on a plate.

6. Put the tofu skin in a bowl and add the edamame, mustard greens, reserved stems, and eggs. Add the dressing, toss to combine, and serve.

Continued

Tofu Skin

Wafer-thin dried tofu skins, also called yuba or bean curd sheets, are flat sheets of bean curd skimmed off during the making of soy milk. Look for flat cellophane packages of them in the noodle section of Chinese markets. When soaked briefly in hot water and stirred, the sheets instantly break apart into rough pasta-like shards. The flavor and texture are so soothing, I sometimes eat tofu skin like porridge for breakfast with milk and maple syrup.

Vietnamese-Style Tofu Salad

—

SERVES 4

Marinade

2 tablespoons mirin

2 tablespoons sambal oelek

3 tablespoons seasoned rice vinegar

4½ teaspoons flavorless vegetable oil

1 tablespoon tamari

1 tablespoon honey

One 14-ounce block firm tofu

1 English (seedless) cucumber

Carrot-Daikon Pickle (recipe follows)

2 Fresno chiles, or other medium-hot red chile, thinly sliced

¼ cup fresh cilantro sprigs

1 tablespoon black sesame seeds, lightly toasted

Rice vinegar to taste

Kosher salt

Lively and a little spicy, this meatless dish satisfies, for lunch or dinner.

1. Marinate the tofu: Whisk all the ingredients for the marinade together in a bowl. Transfer to a covered container or a plastic storage bag. Add the tofu and turn it over several times so it is well coated. Cover or seal and refrigerate for at least 1 day, and up to 5 days—the longer the better—turning the tofu (or bag) occasionally.

2. Preheat the oven to 425°F.

3. Set the tofu on a sheet pan, reserving any excess marinade. Swipe the tofu around to grease the pan. Cut the tofu block horizontally in half, then cut the still-stacked halves into quarters. Cut the quarters in half to form triangles and spread them out on the pan.

4. Baste the tops with the reserved marinade and bake for 12 to 15 minutes, until slightly crisp around the edges. Let cool, then transfer to a wide serving bowl.

5. Meanwhile, cut the cucumbers crosswise into quarters. Stand each quarter on one end and slice into sticks.

6. Drain the carrot-daikon pickle, reserving the liquid, and add to the tofu. Add the cucumber, Fresno chiles, cilantro, and sesame seeds and toss gently together, taking care not to break up the tofu. Drizzle with a tablespoon or so each of reserved pickling liquid and rice vinegar and sprinkle with salt to taste. Serve.

Continued

CARROT-DAIKON PICKLE

MAKES ½ CUP

¼ cup julienned carrot, preferably cut lengthwise on a mandoline

¼ cup julienned daikon, preferably cut lengthwise on a mandoline

¼ cup rice vinegar

¼ cup sugar

A pinch of kosher salt

1. Combine the carrot and daikon in a small heatproof bowl.

2. Combine the rice vinegar, sugar, and salt in a small saucepan and bring to a boil over medium heat. Boil gently, stirring occasionally, for a minute or two, until the sugar is dissolved. Pour the brine over the vegetables and steep until cool. Use right away or store refrigerated in the brine in a tightly covered container for up to 2 weeks.

NOW YOU KNOW

Reusing Pickling Brine

Whether it is one you made yourself or left over from a jar of pickles you purchased, pickling brine can be reused. Just strain out any bits of old vegetable and boil the liquid before pouring over your fresh prepared vegetables. If reusing the brine from a strongly flavored vegetable (onion, daikon radish), it is best to use it only for pickling that same vegetable again.

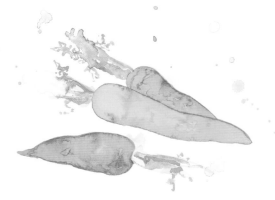

Smoked Trout and Pumpernickel Bread Salad

—

SERVES 4

Mustard Horseradish Dressing

3 tablespoons whole-grain Dijon mustard

3 tablespoons Dijon mustard

3 tablespoons prepared horseradish

2 teaspoons cider vinegar

½ cup flavorless vegetable oil

½ cup water

6 ounces smoked trout fillet

1 small head of escarole (about 4 ounces), separated into leaves, washed, and dried

One 1-pound loaf pumpernickel bread, cut into ¾-inch cubes and dried out overnight

1 English (seedless) cucumber, cut into 1-inch wedges

1 red apple, such as Fuji or Gala

½ cup thinly sliced red onion

1 cup packed torn fresh dill sprigs

8 ounces (1 cup) crème fraîche

This bread salad combines all the flavors of the Sunday smoked-fish breakfasts of my childhood (and adulthood). Pumpernickel croutons stand in for the bagels, and crème fraîche takes the place of the traditional cream cheese.

1. Make the dressing: Combine the mustards, horseradish, and vinegar in the bowl of a food processor or in a blender and pulse to combine. With the motor running, gradually add the oil, and then the water, processing until the dressing is creamy. Set aside.

2. With your fingers, break up the smoked trout into small bite-size pieces. Set aside.

3. Tear the escarole leaves into bite-size pieces. Place in a large bowl, add the bread cubes and cucumber, and toss well.

4. Slice the apple into ¼-inch pieces (see Quick Cut on the following page) and toss with a bit of the dressing to prevent darkening.

5. Add the rest of the dressing, the apple, and the red onion to the salad and toss thoroughly to combine, making sure all the bread is moistened. Add the smoked trout and dill and toss again gently. Transfer to a serving bowl and bring to the table, with the crème fraîche on the side.

Continued

Neatly Slicing an Apple

Cutting off the core at an angle evens up the look of all your apple slices.

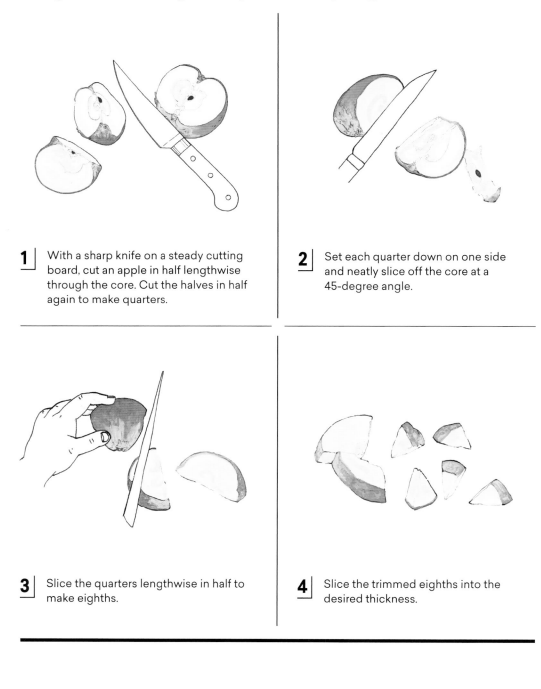

1 With a sharp knife on a steady cutting board, cut an apple in half lengthwise through the core. Cut the halves in half again to make quarters.

2 Set each quarter down on one side and neatly slice off the core at a 45-degree angle.

3 Slice the quarters lengthwise in half to make eighths.

4 Slice the trimmed eighths into the desired thickness.

New Potatoes with Soft Green Herbs

SERVES 4

Lemon-Scallion Yogurt Dressing

2 scallions, roughly chopped

½ cup plain yogurt

Grated zest and juice of 1 lemon

2 tablespoons extra-virgin olive oil

Kosher salt and freshly ground black pepper

1½ pounds small new potatoes, scrubbed

Kosher salt and freshly ground black pepper

About 2 cups mixed fresh herbs (see headnote)

When spring's herbs are at their best, don't mess with them—don't mince them, don't chop them, don't even wash them! Use any combination of whole mint leaves, small dill and/or tarragon sprigs, lovage or celery leaves (torn if large), and long cuts of chives.

1. Make the dressing: Put the scallions in the bowl of a food processor or in a blender, add the yogurt and lemon zest and juice, and pulse to combine. With the motor still running, drizzle in the olive oil and process until smooth. Season to taste with salt and pepper. Set aside.

2. Put the potatoes in a large saucepan, add salted water to cover by 2 inches, and bring to a gentle boil. When the potatoes are just tender enough to be pierced through easily with the tip of a sharp knife, 10 to 12 minutes depending on size, drain in a colander.

3. When the potatoes are cool enough to handle, cut them in half and transfer to a bowl. Add half of the dressing and toss gently, taking care not to break the potatoes. Season to taste with salt and pepper. Let the potatoes cool completely.

4. When ready to serve, add three-quarters of the herbs, including the lovage (or celery leaves), and the remaining dressing to the potatoes and toss to combine. Shower the salad with the remaining herbs.

It's All Green

SERVES 6 TO 8

Kosher salt

8 ounces green beans and/or sugar snap peas, trimmed, any strings removed

8 ounces asparagus, trimmed, tough stalks peeled

6 ounces zucchini, ends trimmed

2 large celery stalks

6 ounces Belgian endives

6 ounces fennel bulbs

Some or All of the Following

Cucumber Shallot Dip (recipe follows)

Pumpkin Seed Hummus (recipe follows)

Avocado Mint Dip (recipe follows)

Cilantro Cumin Dip (recipe follows)

Sweet Lime Salt (recipe follows)

Choose whichever vegetables look beautiful. The amounts of each given here are merely a suggestion. You want approximately 3 to 4 pounds of whole vegetables for six people, and two or three dips to serve on the side, more if you are feeling green.

1. Bring a large pot of salted water to a rolling boil and ready a large bowl of ice water.

2. Add the green beans and/or snap peas to the boiling water and blanch just until they turn bright green. Remove them with a spider or large slotted spoon and transfer to the ice water. Return the water in the pot to a boil and repeat with the asparagus, blanching until just tender, about 2 minutes depending on thickness, before transferring to the ice water. Set aside.

3. Cut the zucchini lengthwise in half, lay flat on a cutting board, and slice on the diagonal into ½-inch pieces.

4. Trim off and discard the ends of the celery stalks and cut the stalks crosswise into thirds. Cut the thirds lengthwise into thin sticks.

5. Trim the bottoms of the endives and separate the leaves; trim the bottoms further if necessary to separate all the leaves.

6. Trim the root ends of the fennel and cut off the stalks, reserving any nice fronds to decorate the platter. Cut the bulbs lengthwise in half, then cut the halves into thin wedges.

7. Arrange all the vegetables on large platters or trays and serve with the dips, hummus, and sweet lime salt.

CUCUMBER SHALLOT DIP

—

MAKES ABOUT 1½ CUPS

1 cup diced English (seedless) cucumber

1½ teaspoons fish sauce

1 tablespoon rice vinegar

1 tablespoon flavorless vegetable oil

2 teaspoons fresh lime juice

2 tablespoons chopped fresh Thai basil, or regular basil

½ cup finely minced shallots

2 tablespoons minced fresh chives

Combine the cucumber, fish sauce, rice vinegar, oil, lime juice, and basil in the bowl of a food processor or in a blender and pulse to puree, scraping down the sides as necessary. Transfer to a small serving bowl and fold in the minced shallots and chives. Cover and refrigerate until ready to serve.

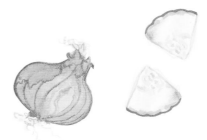

PUMPKIN SEED HUMMUS

—

MAKES ABOUT 2 CUPS

2 cups pumpkin seeds, toasted

2 large garlic cloves

2 tablespoons Dijon mustard

½ cup rice vinegar

¾ cup flavorless vegetable oil

¼ cup hot water, or more if necessary

Kosher salt and freshly ground black pepper

1. Put the pumpkin seeds and garlic in the bowl of a food processor or in a blender and pulse until uniformly ground, scraping down the sides as necessary. The mixture will be rough and sandy looking.

2. Add the mustard and vinegar and pulse to combine. With the motor running, slowly drizzle in the oil, stopping to scrape down the sides of the bowl. Drizzle in the hot water, processing until it is the consistency of thick hummus. Season to taste with salt and pepper. Transfer to a small serving bowl. Cover and refrigerate until ready to serve.

AVOCADO MINT DIP

—

MAKES ABOUT 1¼ CUPS

1 large ripe avocado

5 teaspoons fresh
lemon juice

3 tablespoons chopped
fresh mint leaves

A pinch of cayenne pepper

5 tablespoons water

Pit the avocado and scoop the flesh into the bowl of a food processor or into a blender. Add the lemon juice, mint, and cayenne and pulse to puree, pouring in the water as you go. Transfer to a small serving bowl. Cover and refrigerate until ready to serve.

CILANTRO CUMIN DIP

—

MAKES ABOUT 1½ CUPS

½ cup flavorless
vegetable oil

5 teaspoons cumin seeds

2½ cups chopped
fresh cilantro leaves

3 tablespoons rice vinegar

1 tablespoon seasoned
rice vinegar

2 teaspoons Dijon mustard

1. Pour the oil into a small saucepan and add the cumin seeds. Bring to a simmer over medium heat and simmer gently for 10 minutes. Let cool.

2. Put the cilantro, vinegars, and mustard in the bowl of a food processor or in a blender and pulse to combine. With the motor running, drizzle in the cumin oil and seeds until the mixture is emulsified. Transfer to a small serving bowl. Cover and refrigerate until ready to serve.

SWEET LIME SALT

—

MAKES ABOUT ¾ CUP

¼ cup kosher salt

½ cup sugar

3 limes

1. Mix the salt and sugar together in a small bowl. Zest the limes directly into the salt-sugar mixture. Using your fingers, rub the sugar and salt into the lime zest, grinding it finer. Transfer to a tightly sealed container and refrigerate until ready to serve.

2. Serve the lime salt in a ramekin with a demitasse spoon.

Sweet
Lime Salt

Cilantro
Cumin Dip

Pumpkin Seed
Hummus

Cucumber
Shallot Dip

Avocado
Mint Dip

A (Mostly) Make-Ahead Brunch Menu

This is a fun and unusual way to offer guests the traditional flavors of brunch while getting extra mileage out of your smoked fish budget. Make the Savory Granola and pumpernickel croutons for the bread salad ahead of time, set a pot of coffee before you go to sleep, and this menu will come together almost effortlessly. Double, triple, or quadruple recipes as necessary to feed your crowd.

—

MAKE THIS:

Every-Leafy-Green-You-Can-Find Salad (page 37)

Smoked Trout and Pumpernickel Bread Salad (page 49)

ADD THIS:

Savory Granola (opposite) with fresh fruit, a selection of yogurts, and milk

Hard-Boiled Eggs with Green Olive Mayonnaise (opposite)

BUY THIS:

Babka, muffins, and/or scones

A bottle of your favorite Bloody Mary mix and a liter of vodka

Savory Granola

—

MAKES ABOUT 7 CUPS

Preheat the oven to 350°F. In a large bowl, combine 3 cups old-fashioned rolled oats, 1 cup coarsely chopped walnuts, 1½ cups pumpkin seeds, ¾ cup unsweetened coconut flakes, ¼ cup white sesame seeds, 2 teaspoons kosher salt, ½ teaspoon chile flakes, ¼ teaspoon freshly ground black pepper, ½ cup plus 2 tablespoons maple syrup, and ½ cup extra-virgin olive oil. Toss thoroughly and spread out on a parchment-lined sheet pan. Toast, stirring and turning often, for 25 to 30 minutes, until golden brown and crisp. Cool completely before transferring to tightly lidded jars. The granola keeps for 2 weeks on the shelf or for a month in the refrigerator.

Hard-Boiled Eggs with Green Olive Mayonnaise

—

MAKES ENOUGH FOR 6 EGGS

First, make the green olive mayonnaise: Spoon ¾ cup mayonnaise into a small bowl. Drain 2 ounces pitted green olives, reserving a tablespoon of the brine, and chop fine. Stir into the mayonnaise, blending well. Stir in olive brine to taste. Transfer to a small serving bowl and refrigerate, covered with plastic wrap, until serving time. (The mayonnaise can be made up to 1 week ahead.)

Place 6 eggs in a pot, cover with several inches of cold water, and bring to a boil over high heat. Cover the pot, turn off the heat, and let stand for at least 10 minutes. When the eggs are cool enough to handle, remove from the pot. Crack the shell of each egg at the wide end and peel it (under cool running water if the shells are sticking). If not serving in the next hour or so, refrigerate. Serve accompanied by the green olive mayonnaise.

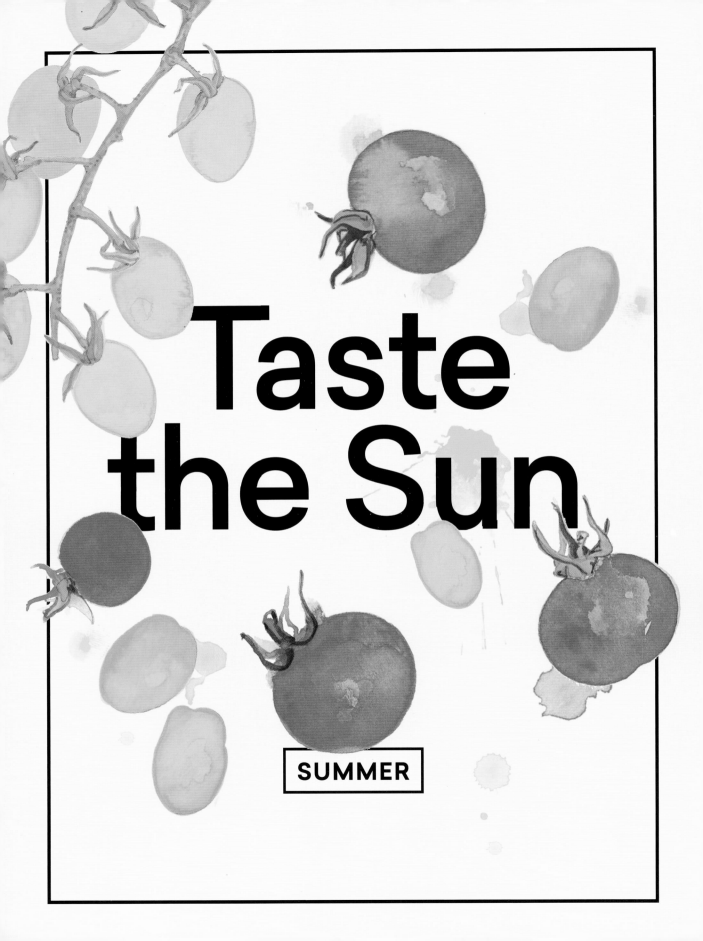

Taste
the Sun

SUMMER

Summer is a barrage of multicolored goodness, everything at its peak. Heaps of fruits and vegetables—a spontaneous still life yielding simple, bright meals.

Tomato Wedges, Lemon Onions, and Bok Choy

—

SERVES 4

Lemon Onions

2 medium onions, sliced ⅛ inch thick

2 teaspoons grated lemon zest

3 tablespoons fresh lemon juice

4 teaspoons extra-virgin olive oil

Kosher salt and freshly ground black pepper

1 pound small tomatoes

Kosher salt

1 pound baby or regular bok choy, trimmed and cut crosswise into ribbons

¼ cup extra-virgin olive oil, or to taste

Freshly ground black pepper

Lemon onions are a revelation: They're easy to make and add a bright, piquant flavor to anything from a cheese sandwich to a grilled steak. Try this with other citrus as well—simply replace the zest and juice of the lemon with lime or orange. Note that the onions need to be marinated in the refrigerator overnight before serving.

If you can find young purple bok choy, grab it—the color contrasts beautifully with the bright red tomatoes.

1. Make the lemon onions: Combine the onions, lemon zest, lemon juice, and olive oil in a bowl and mix thoroughly. Season to taste with salt and pepper. Refrigerate overnight to mellow the onions.

2. Cut the tomatoes into wedges, sprinkle with salt to taste, and arrange in a shallow serving bowl. Add the bok choy and lemon onions and toss well. Drizzle with the olive oil and toss again gently. Season to taste with salt and pepper, drizzle with more olive oil if desired, and serve.

MORE USES FOR LEMON ONIONS

- As a garnish for avocado toasts

- Pureed with butter to slather on corn on the cob

- Mixed with olive oil to make a marinade for cubed feta

- As a topping for lamb burgers

Smoky, Spicy Okra and Cherry Tomatoes

SERVES 4

1½ pounds okra

⅓ cup canned chipotle chiles in adobo, with some of their sauce

⅓ cup flavorless vegetable oil

Kosher salt and freshly ground black pepper

2 pints cherry tomatoes

Crack open a can of chiles in adobo and take your okra south of the border!

1. Preheat the oven to 400°F.

2. Trim the tips of the stems of the okra; do not cut the whole stem off. Transfer to a medium bowl.

3. Put the chiles and their sauce in the bowl of a food processor or in a blender and pulse to puree. Add the oil and pulse until blended.

4. Pour the mixture over the okra, season to taste with salt and pepper, and toss well. Spread the okra out on a sheet pan and roast for about 15 minutes, until the pods are crisped and tender but have not burst.

5. Meanwhile, arrange the cherry tomatoes on a sheet pan and set it in the oven with the okra. Roast until the tomatoes soften and start to brown, about 12 minutes. Transfer to a bowl and season to taste with salt and pepper while still hot.

6. When the okra is done, add it to the bowl of tomatoes, scraping up the crisp chile bits from the pan and adding them to the bowl as well. Toss to combine. Taste again, adjust the seasoning if necessary, and serve.

Choose-Your-Style Tiny Tomatoes

—

SERVES 4

12 ounces mixed tiny
tomatoes (see headnote)

Kosher salt and freshly
ground black pepper

At the peak of summer, when field-grown cherry, grape, and pear tomatoes appear in myriad colors and shapes, all bursting with flavor. They are impossible to resist—buy them all. *Vivid & Surprising Style pictured on page 6.*

START HERE

1. Halve the tomatoes: Cut round tomatoes in half across the equator for a prettier face, and halve oval and pear-shaped tomatoes lengthwise to preserve their elegant lines. Combine all the tomatoes in a bowl.

2. Season with salt and pepper to taste, then choose your style from the chart on the opposite page to complete the dish, toss, and serve.

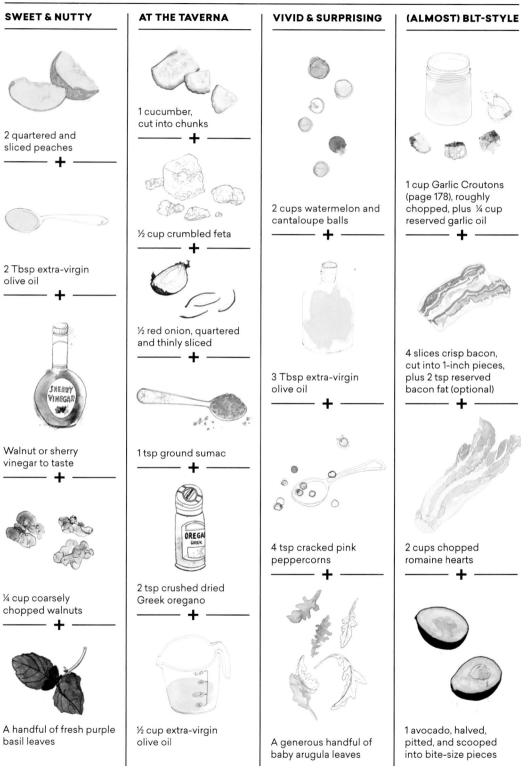

SWEET & NUTTY	AT THE TAVERNA	VIVID & SURPRISING	(ALMOST) BLT-STYLE
2 quartered and sliced peaches	1 cucumber, cut into chunks	2 cups watermelon and cantaloupe balls	1 cup Garlic Croutons (page 178), roughly chopped, plus ¼ cup reserved garlic oil
+	+	+	+
2 Tbsp extra-virgin olive oil	½ cup crumbled feta	3 Tbsp extra-virgin olive oil	4 slices crisp bacon, cut into 1-inch pieces, plus 2 tsp reserved bacon fat (optional)
+	+	+	+
Walnut or sherry vinegar to taste	½ red onion, quartered and thinly sliced	4 tsp cracked pink peppercorns	2 cups chopped romaine hearts
+	+	+	+
¼ cup coarsely chopped walnuts	1 tsp ground sumac	A generous handful of baby arugula leaves	1 avocado, halved, pitted, and scooped into bite-size pieces
+	+		
A handful of fresh purple basil leaves	2 tsp crushed dried Greek oregano		
	+		
	½ cup extra-virgin olive oil		

Really Yellow

SERVES 4

Lemongrass Mayonnaise

3 or 4 stalks fresh lemongrass (depending on size)

1 cup flavorless vegetable oil

2 large egg yolks, at room temperature

2 teaspoons Dijon mustard, at room temperature

Kosher salt

4 slices ripe yellow beefsteak tomato (about ½ inch thick)

Kosher salt

4 Six-Minute Eggs (recipe follows), cooled

Flaky salt and cracked black pepper

A handful of fresh lemon basil leaves, or regular basil

2 radishes, cut into matchsticks

¼ cup diced celery

4 slices white or sourdough bread, toasted and cut into triangles

Egg salad, long a staple for ladies who lunch, gets a makeover in this deconstructed version. (We've kept the toast points.)

1. Make the lemongrass oil for the mayonnaise: Trim off the tough outer leaves of the lemongrass to expose the tender centers. Cut them into 1-inch lengths, bruise them with a rolling pin or meat pounder to release their fragrant oils, and slice thin.

2. Combine the lemongrass and oil in a small saucepan and heat over medium heat just until the oil comes to a boil. Reduce the heat to a bare simmer and simmer for 5 minutes to infuse the oil. Turn off the heat and allow the oil to steep for 30 minutes, then strain and let cool to room temperature.

3. Make the mayonnaise: Whisk the egg yolks and mustard together with a pinch of salt in a medium bowl until thick and creamy. Slowly whisk in the lemongrass oil, a few drops at a time at first, until the mixture begins to emulsify, then continue whisking in the oil in a slow, steady stream until the mayonnaise is thick and shiny and all the oil has been absorbed. Check the seasoning and add more salt if necessary. Cover and refrigerate until serving time.

Continued

NOW YOU KNOW

Lemongrass Substitute

If you don't have lemongrass, a teaspoon of lime zest mixed with a tablespoon of lemon zest makes a decent stand-in. In this case, you won't need to simmer it; just mix the zests with the oil for the mayonnaise.

4. Divide the tomato slices among four plates, sprinkle them with kosher salt, and spoon a generous dollop of mayonnaise onto each slice (you should have some left over). Set each egg on a tomato slice, nestling it into the mayonnaise. Sprinkle each plate with flaky salt, cracked black pepper, and basil leaves. Scatter the radish sticks and diced celery over the top.

5. Serve with the toast triangles and the remaining mayonnaise on the side.

SIX-MINUTE EGGS

—

SERVES 4

4 large eggs (plus a few extra, just in case), at room temperature

This just-soft-enough egg holds its shape but is still creamy inside. Surprisingly, it can even be made ahead and rewarmed, and that perfect texture remains.

1. Bring a large pot of water to a rolling boil over high heat and ready a large bowl of ice water. To ensure that the eggs cook evenly, use a spider or a small colander to lower all the eggs at once into the boiling water. Remove after exactly 6 minutes and immediately plunge into the ice water.

2. When the eggs have cooled enough to handle, remove them from the ice water. Carefully crack the shell of each egg at the wider end (where the air pocket is) and begin to peel from there, as patiently as possible. If a few of the eggs look a little rough, eat them yourself or refrigerate for another time.

3. If not using them right away, refrigerate the peeled eggs until ready to serve. If desired, reheat them by sliding them into a hot water bath for about 2 minutes, until warm to the touch.

Tex-Mex Cornbread Salad

SERVES 4

Cornbread

3 tablespoons unsalted butter, melted, plus more for the pan

1 cup cornmeal

½ cup all-purpose flour

2 tablespoons sugar

2 teaspoons baking powder

½ teaspoon baking soda

1 teaspoon kosher salt

2 cups buttermilk

2 large eggs, lightly beaten

Mexican Oregano Vinaigrette

¼ cup seasoned rice vinegar

2 tablespoons Dijon mustard

4 teaspoons dried Mexican oregano

1 cup flavorless vegetable oil

Kosher salt and freshly ground black pepper

8 ounces pepper Jack cheese, cut into ⅓-inch cubes

2 cups cherry tomatoes, halved

Kosher salt (optional)

2 handfuls (about 5 ounces) of purslane, torn into sprigs, or spinach, stems trimmed

½ cup pumpkin seeds, toasted

½ cup chopped scallions

When crisp cornbread croutons are soaked in a woodsy Mexican oregano vinaigrette, the two ingredients combine to become something else entirely. Studded with cherry tomatoes, creamy pepper Jack cheese, and juicy leaves of purslane, the resulting salad is rich and savory.

1. Make the cornbread: Preheat the oven to 375°F. Generously butter a 9-inch square cake pan.

2. Whisk the dry ingredients together in a large bowl. Lightly whisk together the buttermilk, eggs, and melted butter in a small bowl, then stir into the dry ingredients to blend.

3. Pour the batter into the buttered pan and spread it evenly with a rubber spatula. Bake for 12 to 15 minutes, until the top is golden brown and the edges pull away from the sides of the pan; a toothpick poked into the center should come out clean. Remove from the oven, but leave the oven on. Cool slightly on a rack, then unmold onto the rack and cool for 10 to 15 minutes.

4. Cut the cornbread into 1-inch cubes and spread them out on a sheet pan. Return to the oven and bake for about 10 minutes, turning occasionally, until all the edges are crisp and toasted. Transfer to another sheet pan to cool.

Continued

NOW YOU KNOW

Buttermilk Substitutes

Don't have buttermilk on hand? As an alternative to 1 cup buttermilk, pour 1½ tablespoons white vinegar or lemon juice into a measuring cup and add enough milk to measure 1 cup. Let stand for 5 minutes. Or whisk ½ cup milk into ½ cup plain yogurt and let stand for 5 minutes before using.

5. Make the vinaigrette: Put the vinegar, mustard, and oregano in the bowl of a food processor or in a blender and pulse to combine. With the motor running, drizzle in the oil until the mixture is emulsified. Season to taste with salt and pepper.

6. Put the cornbread cubes, cheese, and cherry tomatoes in a large bowl. Pour three-quarters of the vinaigrette over them and toss thoroughly. Check the seasoning and add salt if necessary. Toss the greens separately with the remaining dressing.

7. Layer the cornbread mixture into a wide bowl with the dressed greens and 6 tablespoons each of the pumpkin seeds and scallions. Scatter the remaining 2 tablespoons each seeds and scallions over the top. Serve.

MEET THE INGREDIENT

Purslane

Typically used in Mexican cooking, purslane is a succulent (literally!) counterpoint to other leafy greens, and a great addition to any taco. The juicy leaves and stems stand up well to the croutons in this salad.

Choose-Your-Style Japanese Eggplant Boats

—

2 Japanese eggplants
of the same size (about
6 ounces each)

1 tablespoon flavorless
vegetable oil

Kosher salt and freshly
ground black pepper

Japanese eggplants, split lengthwise and roasted, make festive "boats" when painted with a dressing (or yogurt) and decorated with confetti-like toppings. Choose just one style, or make several for a party. *Flecked Style pictured on page 9.*

START HERE

1. Preheat the oven to 400°F.

2. Cut the eggplants lengthwise in half and arrange skin side down on a sheet pan. Score the cut surfaces in a crosshatch pattern with a sharp knife. Brush generously with the oil and sprinkle with salt and pepper to taste.

3. Roast the eggplants for about 18 minutes, until lightly browned and almost completely tender. Remove from the oven, paint generously with the dressing or yogurt for your chosen style (opposite), and return to the oven until the tops are caramelized.

4. Transfer the eggplant to a serving platter. Decorate with the designated toppings for your chosen style. Season to taste with more salt and pepper if necessary and serve warm or at room temperature.

CHOOSE YOUR STYLE

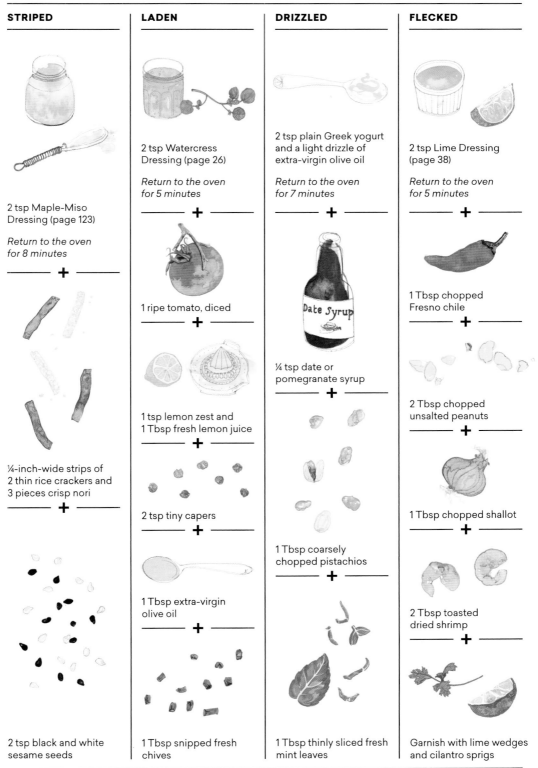

STRIPED	LADEN	DRIZZLED	FLECKED
2 tsp Maple-Miso Dressing (page 123) *Return to the oven for 8 minutes* **+** ¼-inch-wide strips of 2 thin rice crackers and 3 pieces crisp nori **+** 2 tsp black and white sesame seeds	2 tsp Watercress Dressing (page 26) *Return to the oven for 5 minutes* **+** 1 ripe tomato, diced **+** 1 tsp lemon zest and 1 Tbsp fresh lemon juice **+** 2 tsp tiny capers **+** 1 Tbsp extra-virgin olive oil **+** 1 Tbsp snipped fresh chives	2 tsp plain Greek yogurt and a light drizzle of extra-virgin olive oil *Return to the oven for 7 minutes* **+** ¼ tsp date or pomegranate syrup **+** 1 Tbsp coarsely chopped pistachios **+** 1 Tbsp thinly sliced fresh mint leaves	2 tsp Lime Dressing (page 38) *Return to the oven for 5 minutes* **+** 1 Tbsp chopped Fresno chile **+** 2 Tbsp chopped unsalted peanuts **+** 1 Tbsp chopped shallot **+** 2 Tbsp toasted dried shrimp **+** Garnish with lime wedges and cilantro sprigs

Watermelon with Chrysanthemum and Shiso

—

SERVES 4

4 large wedges seedless watermelon, rind removed and flesh cut into triangles (see Quick Cut on the following page), about 8 cups

8 ounces ricotta salata, cut into matchsticks

1 bunch of chrysanthemum leaves or baby arugula

A handful of shiso leaves or baby arugula

¼ cup pumpkin seeds, toasted

Kosher salt and freshly ground black pepper

Extra-virgin olive oil for drizzling

Come summertime, I can't get enough watermelon. When I tire of pairing it with the usual mint and feta, I seek out chrysanthemum greens and shiso leaves, which impart magical herbal notes. If you can't find either of them, you can substitute arugula.

Arrange the watermelon on a platter or on individual serving dishes. Scatter the cheese strips and greens over the watermelon and sprinkle with the pumpkin seeds. Sprinkle with salt and pepper to taste and finish with a generous drizzle of olive oil.

Continued

MEET THE INGREDIENTS

Chrysanthemum Leaves and Shiso

Chrysanthemum leaves are much appreciated in Japan and other parts of Asia for their grassy, floral flavor. Shiso leaves are the saw-toothed oval leaves you find on your sushi platter, and I hope you've been eating them all these years, because they are delicious. Both are standouts in salads. Find them at Asian markets or farmers' markets.

Breaking Down a Watermelon

For a more elegant presentation than random chunks:

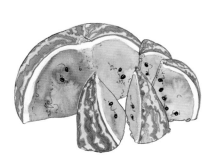

1 | Cut the watermelon crosswise in half. Lay it cut side down. Cut each piece in half again. Cut each section into 4 to 6 wedges, depending on size.

2 | Lay each wedge down flat on the board. With a narrow, flexible knife such as a utility knife, cut the flesh from the rind, following the curve.

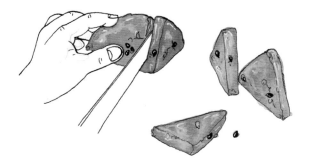

3 | While it's still flat on the board, slice the rindless melon wedge ½ inch thick, to form graduated triangles.

Charred Summer Squash with Spicy Cucumbers

—

SERVES 4

1½ pounds mixed
small summer squash,
such as pattypan, globe,
and small zucchini

4 teaspoons flavorless
vegetable oil, plus more for
brushing

Kosher salt

2 tablespoons gochujang
(see page 17)

2 Persian or Kirby
cucumbers

1 large shallot

1 tablespoon seasoned
rice vinegar

½ to 1 teaspoon gochugaru
flakes (see page 17)

Flaky salt

Here's a recipe for a medley of summer squashes for those days when it's impossible to choose just one. Gochujang, Korean chile paste, adds savory heat, while the cucumbers spiked with gochugaru (chile flakes) cool and tingle the palate at the same time.

1. Cut the squash lengthwise in half. If using slightly larger globe squashes, cut them into quarters. With a sharp knife, score a crosshatch pattern in the cut surfaces, then brush lightly with oil and sprinkle with kosher salt.

2. Mix together the gochujang and 2 teaspoons of the oil in a small bowl.

3. Slice the cucumber and shallot very thin on a mandoline and transfer to a bowl. Toss with the rice vinegar and the gochugaru flakes and kosher salt to taste.

4. Heat a 10-inch cast-iron skillet over high heat for several minutes, until a drop of water skitters across the surface. Brush with 2 teaspoons of the remaining oil and, when it starts to smoke, add an uncrowded layer of the squash cut side down. Cook the larger pieces for 8 to 10 minutes, until evenly charred but not outright burnt. If the pan gets too hot, reduce the heat to medium. Brush the tops of the squash with oil, turn them, and cook for about 5 minutes more, or until tender. If using squash cut into quarters, turn the pieces as necessary to char on all sides. The timing will vary here depending on the thickness of the squash. Repeat with any remaining squash.

5. Transfer the squash to a platter, brush the cut sides with the gochujang and oil mixture, and sprinkle with flaky salt. Serve with the cucumbers on the side.

Zucchini Ribbons with Squash Blossoms

SERVES 4

1 pound young yellow and/
or green zucchini, ends
trimmed

Kosher salt

5 ounces medium-aged
Gouda

6 zucchini blossoms

1 good-size bunch of
dandelion greens, trimmed

3 tablespoons fruity
extra-virgin olive oil,
or more if desired

Pumpkin seed oil for
drizzling (optional)

Freshly ground black
pepper

⅓ cup pumpkin seeds,
toasted

½ cup fresh mint leaves,
thinly sliced into chiffonade
(see Quick Cut, page 29)

To turn this side dish into a satisfying meal for four, echo the ribbon theme by tossing the squash with a pound of fresh pappardelle.

1. Slice the zucchini lengthwise into thin ribbons on a mandoline, discarding the first and last slice. Sprinkle generously with salt, toss, and spread out in a colander. Put over a large bowl or the sink and let drain for about 15 minutes, then pat the ribbons dry.

2. Meanwhile, trim the rind off the cheese and shave the cheese into thin slices with a vegetable peeler (see Quick Cut below).

3. Gently separate the zucchini blossoms into petals.

4. Arrange half of the zucchini ribbons, dandelion greens, zucchini blossoms, and cheese in a layer on a large platter. Drizzle with half of the olive oil and a little pumpkin seed oil, if using. Sprinkle with salt and pepper to taste. Scatter half of the pumpkin seeds and mint over the top. Repeat with a second layer, drizzle with additional olive oil if desired and the pumpkin seed oil if using, and serve immediately.

| QUICK CUT |

Shaving Cheese

A triangular wedge of cheese makes the prettiest slices, but you can use whatever you've got.

1 | Remove the rind.

2 | Using a Y-shaped peeler, shave from the wide end down to the point in one pass.

Potatoes and Cucumbers with Caraway and All Kinds of Mustard

SERVES 4

1½ pounds small red potatoes, scrubbed

Kosher salt

Mustard Caraway Dressing

3 tablespoons whole-grain Dijon mustard

3 tablespoons Dijon mustard

2 tablespoons cider vinegar

1 teaspoon caraway seeds

2 tablespoons flavorless vegetable oil

¾ teaspoon honey

2 tablespoons water

12 ounces small cucumbers, such as lemon, Little Potato, or Kirby, or a combination, cut into small wedges

2 tablespoons capers

2 tablespoon Pickled Mustard Seeds (recipe follows)

⅓ cup small fresh dill sprigs

Freshly ground black pepper

Go wild at the cucumber stand and grab the most interesting cukes you can find!

1. If the potatoes are very small, leave them whole. If they are on the larger side, cut them in half. Place in a pot of cold salted water and bring to a boil over high heat. Reduce the heat and simmer gently for about 10 minutes, until you can pierce the potatoes right through with the sharp point of a knife. Drain. When the potatoes are cool enough to handle, cut any whole potatoes in half and transfer all the potatoes to a large bowl.

2. While the potatoes are cooking, make the dressing: Combine all the ingredients in the bowl of a food processor or in a blender and process until smooth and creamy. Add ½ cup of the dressing and a sprinkling of salt to the warm potatoes and toss gently to coat. Let cool.

3. Add the cucumbers, capers, mustard seeds, and dill to the potatoes. Toss to combine, then add the remaining dressing and toss gently. Season to taste with salt and pepper and serve.

Continued

NOW YOU KNOW

Measuring Honey

To keep honey from sticking to a measuring cup or spoon, swipe the cup or spoon lightly with an oil-dampened paper towel first. I do this for mustard, too.

PICKLED MUSTARD SEEDS

—

MAKES ABOUT ¼ CUP

¼ cup white wine vinegar

¼ cup water

¼ cup sugar

¼ cup mustard seeds
(yellow or brown)

These look like caviar and pop a bit like it, too. They can be made well ahead of time (they keep for weeks in the fridge) and taste great on sandwiches.

Combine the vinegar, water, and sugar in a small saucepan and bring to a gentle boil over medium heat, stirring occasionally, until the sugar is dissolved. Add the mustard seeds and boil for about 5 minutes, until the seeds swell. Remove from the heat and let cool. Store excess mustard seeds in their brine.

Corn × 3

—

SERVES 4

¼ cup cracked dried hominy, picked over, rinsed, and soaked overnight in water to cover

Basil Dressing

½ cup packed fresh basil leaves

2 tablespoons cider vinegar

2¼ teaspoons Dijon mustard

6 tablespoons flavorless vegetable oil

Kosher salt and freshly ground black pepper

2 ears corn, shucked and silks removed

½ cup diced green tomato or tomatillo

¼ cup thinly sliced scallions

1 jalapeño, seeded and chopped

⅓ cup corn nuts or quicos, chopped if large

¼ cup fresh cilantro sprigs

Kosher salt and freshly ground black pepper

Start with the essence of summer, fresh sweet corn, and add hominy (dried corn) for substance and crunchy, salty corn nuts for a concentrated corn flavor.

1. Bring a medium saucepan of water to a boil over medium-high heat. Drain and rinse the hominy, add to the pan, and cook for 20 to 30 minutes, until tender but still slightly chewy. Drain in a colander and let cool, then transfer to a wide bowl and fluff with your fingers to break up any clumps. Set aside.

2. Make the dressing: Put the basil leaves in the bowl of a food processor or in a blender, and pulse several times to chop the basil, scraping down the sides if necessary. Add the cider vinegar and mustard. With the motor running, stream in the oil, processing until the dressing is smooth. Season to taste with salt and pepper.

3. To steam the corn, put the ears in a lidded skillet, add water to come halfway up the sides of the ears, cover the pan, bring to a boil, and boil for 1 minute. Let stand for 5 minutes, then drain and let cool.

4. Cut the corn kernels off the cobs (see Quick Cut on the following page). Add the corn, green tomatoes, scallions, jalapeño, and corn nuts to the hominy and toss well. Add the basil dressing and cilantro, season with salt and pepper to taste, and serve.

Continued

Removing Corn Kernels from the Cob

No more kernels flying all over the counter!

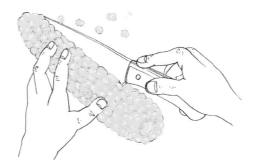

1 Lay a shucked ear of corn on its side on a cutting board.

2 With a sharp chef's knife, cut straight down one side of the ear at the base of the kernels toward the board, releasing the kernels straight onto the board. Turn and repeat with the remaining kernels.

Cucumbers with Black Sesame Seeds and Sweet Lime Vinegar

SERVES 4

1½ pounds English (seedless) cucumbers, sliced about ⅛ inch thick

Kosher salt

¼ cup Sweet Lime Vinegar (recipe follows)

1 tablespoon black sesame seeds, toasted

1 tablespoon fresh lime juice

3 tablespoons fresh tarragon leaves

Bright, refreshing, sweet, and tangy, these cucumbers work just as well next to (or inside) a hearty winter sandwich as they do at a summer barbecue.

Any leftover cucumbers will keep well for a few days in the refrigerator, but they will continue to give off liquid; just drain it off and add another squeeze of fresh lime juice before serving.

1. Sprinkle the cucumber slices with salt, spread them out in a large colander, set it in a large bowl or the sink, and let drain for 30 minutes.

2. Press down on the cucumbers to release as much liquid as you can, then blot them very dry and transfer to a serving bowl. Add the lime vinegar and most of the sesame seeds, reserving some for garnish. Toss to combine and refrigerate until ready to serve. They can remain in the fridge for 2 days or longer.

3. When ready to serve, using a slotted spoon, transfer the cucumbers to a serving bowl; discard the liquid. Add the lime juice and tarragon, toss to combine, and use a fork to separate the cucumbers. Scatter the reserved sesame seeds over the top and serve.

SWEET LIME VINEGAR

MAKES ABOUT ¾ CUP

½ cup rice vinegar

½ cup sugar

Grated zest and juice of 1 large or 2 small limes

1. Bring the vinegar and sugar to a boil in a small saucepan over medium heat, stirring occasionally. Lower the heat and simmer for 2 to 3 minutes, until the sugar is dissolved and the mixture is slightly syrupy.

2. Remove from the heat and stir in the lime zest and half of the juice. Cool enough to taste, then check for limey-ness, adding more juice if necessary. Cool completely before using. The vinegar can be kept for 2 weeks or longer in the fridge.

Tabouleh-esque

SERVES 6 TO 8

Kosher salt

1 cup dried green lentils, picked over and rinsed

1 cup medium (no. 2) bulgur

2 cups boiling water

1 cup lentil sprouts or mixed sprouts, rinsed and dried

8 ounces any combination of medium to large white Japanese turnips and/or watermelon radishes or other radishes, cut into ¼-inch dice (about 2 cups)

1 or 2 small cucumbers, cut into ¼-inch dice (about 1 cup)

4 scallions, chopped

Freshly ground black pepper

¾ cup fresh mint leaves

¾ cup small fresh dill sprigs

¾ cup fresh flat-leaf parsley

6 tablespoons fresh lemon juice (from about 2 lemons)

½ cup fruity extra-virgin olive oil, or to taste

Here lentils combine with bulgur to make a nourishing salad with plenty of herbs and crisp vegetables. I always make a lot of this, because it's going to taste *at least* as good the next day.

1. Bring a large pot of salted water to a boil and add the lentils. Reduce the heat to medium-low and simmer for about 20 minutes, until the lentils are tender but not mushy. Drain and let cool; add salt to taste.

2. Meanwhile, put the bulgur in a medium heatproof bowl and pour the 2 cups boiling water over it. Let stand for 30 minutes.

3. Drain the bulgur in a fine-mesh strainer, press out the excess liquid, and transfer to a wide serving bowl. Season with salt to taste.

4. Add the cooled lentils, the sprouts, and all the vegetables to the bulgur. Toss to combine and season with salt and pepper. Reserve ¼ cup mixed herbs for the garnish, and add the rest of the herbs to the bowl. Add the lemon juice and olive oil, toss again gently, and check the seasoning. Add more olive oil if desired. Top with the reserved herbs and serve.

NOW YOU KNOW

Reviving a Day-Old Grain Salad

Three things will usually make your leftovers as good as new: (1) picking out any wilted herbs or leaves and replacing them with fresh ones, (2) adding a little reserved dressing or olive oil, and (3) adding more salt to taste. Then toss and enjoy again!

Three-Bean Salad (Kinda)

—

SERVES 4

Adzuki Dressing

¼ cup adzuki bean miso

1 tablespoon seasoned rice vinegar

1½ teaspoons Dijon mustard

5 tablespoons flavorless vegetable oil

1½ pounds green beans, trimmed

Kosher salt

¼ cup drained red mung beans preserved in sugar syrup

In this Asian twist on an old-time standard, the third bean is actually in the dressing: adzuki bean miso adds a salty, fermented kick. I especially like South River brand.

1. Make the dressing: Whisk together the miso, rice vinegar, and mustard in a small bowl. Gradually whisk in the oil until thoroughly blended.

2. Bring a large pot of salted water to a rolling boil; ready a large bowl of ice water. Add the green beans to the boiling water and cook for several minutes, until just tender. Drain and transfer to the ice water. Drain again, pat dry, and cut in half.

3. Toss the green beans and half the mung beans with the dressing in a medium bowl; taste and add salt if desired. Top with remaining mung beans and serve.

MEET THE INGREDIENT

Preserved Mung Beans

Filipino preserved mung beans, sold in jars in Asian markets, add a surprising sweetness (think Japanese or Chinese red bean paste desserts). Try stirring a few spoonfuls into steamed jasmine or brown rice.

Tofu Shirataki Noodles with Spicy Thai Basil Pesto

—

SERVES 6

Spicy Thai Basil Pesto

2 cups fresh Thai basil leaves, or substitute half regular basil and half mint leaves

¼ cup unsalted peanuts

1 fresh Thai bird or other hot chile, seeded and minced, or to taste

½ cup flavorless vegetable oil

Kosher salt and freshly ground black pepper

A few drops of fish sauce (optional)

½ cup dried shrimp

1½ pounds wide shirataki noodles

Kosher salt

¼ cup unsalted peanuts

½ cup fresh Thai basil leaves, or half regular basil and half mint leaves

The classic Italian pasta-and-pesto template is made new with Thai basil and peanuts, shirataki noodles, and funky dried shrimp. You'll find the noodles next to tofu products in the refrigerator case in Asian markets and some supermarkets; don't be intimidated—the slippery tofu noodles are fun and quick to prepare.

1. Make the pesto: Put the basil leaves in the bowl of a food processor or in a blender and pulse to chop, scraping down the sides as necessary. Add the peanuts and the hot chile and process to combine, scraping down the sides. With the motor running, drizzle in the oil, processing until smooth. Season to taste with salt and pepper and, if desired, the fish sauce. Set aside.

2. Toast the dried shrimp in a small dry skillet over medium heat for about a minute, until fragrant. Transfer to a plate.

3. Bring a large pot of water to a boil. Put the noodles in a colander and rinse well under cold running water. Add to the boiling water and cook for 2 minutes, or until heated through. Drain and transfer to a large bowl.

4. Toss the noodles with the pesto. Add salt to taste and toss again. Add the shrimp and peanuts and toss again lightly. Transfer to a serving bowl, shower the basil leaves over the top, and serve.

NOW YOU KNOW

Toasting Tiny Items

Nuts, seeds, or the dried shrimp called for in this recipe can be toasted until crisp and fragrant in a small skillet over low to medium heat, on a small baking sheet in a toaster oven, or in a moderate oven if it's already on. Watch carefully, since things can quickly go from toasted to burnt!

Chilled Soba and Smoked Salmon in Yuzu Kosho Broth

—

SERVES 4

4 small white Japanese turnips, trimmed

4 ounces thinly sliced smoked salmon

Yuzu Kosho Broth

2 teaspoons yuzu kosho (see page 18)

5 teaspoons mirin

¾ teaspoon toasted sesame oil

1 teaspoon rice vinegar

¾ teaspoon tamari

1 teaspoon grated fresh ginger

¼ teaspoon grated orange zest

1 bunch of mustard greens, other Asian greens, or spinach, thick stems removed

One 300-gram package of buckwheat soba noodles

2 teaspoons black sesame seeds, toasted

2 teaspoons white sesame seeds, toasted

4 scallions, sliced on the diagonal

Yuzu kosho—a Japanese seasoning paste—makes for a spicy, citrusy broth here, which plays off the richness of the smoked salmon.

1. Slice the turnips about ¼ inch thick, then stack the slices and cut into ¼-inch-thick matchsticks. Set aside.

2. Slice the smoked salmon into ¼-inch-wide strips. Refrigerate until ready to serve.

3. Make the broth: Combine all the ingredients in a heatproof bowl.

4. Bring a large pot of water to a boil. When it's almost boiling, scoop out 2 cups of the hot water, pour over the broth ingredients, and stir to blend. Refrigerate until chilled.

5. Bring the water back to a boil. Tie the greens into a bundle with kitchen string and, using tongs, plunge into the boiling water just long enough to wilt the greens, a minute or less. Transfer to a colander, remove the string, and run under cold water until the greens are cool. Roll them in a kitchen towel to dry and place them on one side of a wide shallow bowl.

6. Bring the water back to a boil and add the noodles, stirring to separate them. Cook for about 4 minutes, until they are just tender. Drain in a colander and run under cold water until they are cool. Drain again.

7. Put the noodles in a large bowl, add the turnips, smoked salmon, 1½ teaspoons each of the black and white sesame seeds, and most of the scallions, and toss to combine. Heap the noodles next to the greens.

8. To serve, pour half of the chilled broth over the noodles and greens and top with the remaining seeds and scallions. Set out with tongs and a ladle, individual soup bowls, chopsticks, and spoons. Serve the remaining broth in a pitcher on the side to top up the soup.

A Summer-to-Go Menu

A relaxed menu to serve outside, on a picnic table, the grass, or the sand. Double, triple, or quadruple recipes as necessary to feed your crowd.

—

MAKE THIS:

Tiny Tomatoes, Sweet & Nutty Style (page 68)

Watermelon with Chrysanthemum and Shiso (page 79)

Corn × 3 (page 89)

ADD THIS:

Gruyère and Avocado Sandwiches (opposite)

"Horse and Pig" Sandwiches (opposite)

BUY THIS:

Iced tea and lemonade (spiked or not)

Shortbread cookies

Gruyère and Avocado Sandwiches

—

MAKES 4 SANDWICHES

Spread 8 slices of whole-grain bread with mayonnaise and top each one with a slice of Gruyère cheese. Halve, pit, and slice 1 or 2 avocados and top half of the slices of bread and cheese with them. Sprinkle with lemon juice, olive oil, and salt and pepper. Cover with a layer of alfalfa sprouts, and cut the bread slices in half. Cut the remaining 4 slices of bread and cheese in half, and cover the sandwiches. (Cutting the sandwiches in half before assembling them helps keep the avocado from squishing out.) Arrange the sandwiches on a large platter, cover with plastic wrap, and refrigerate until ready to serve. Or, if transporting them, wrap individually in waxed or parchment paper, tied with bakery string, and refrigerate.

"Horse and Pig" Sandwiches

—

MAKES 4 SANDWICHES

Fry 8 slices of thick-cut bacon until almost crisp, and drain on paper towels. Toast and butter 8 slices of white or sourdough sandwich bread. Spread 4 slices with drained prepared horseradish, drizzle on olive oil, top with a few thin slices of red onion, and sprinkle with salt and pepper. Top each sandwich with 2 pieces of crisp bacon and cover with the remaining bread. Arrange on a large platter, cover with plastic wrap, and refrigerate until ready to serve. Or, if transporting the sandwiches, wrap individually in waxed or parchment paper, tie with string, and refrigerate.

Technicolor Bounty

FALL

Shorter days, cooler evenings, an explosion of scarlet, vermilion, and violet. Use the last of the lettuces and settle in for hard squashes, giant brassicas, roots, and roasting pans.

—

Gem Lettuces, Avocado, and Tomatillo with Buttermilk Dressing

Buttermilk Dressing

1 small garlic clove

¼ teaspoon kosher salt

1½ teaspoons Dijon mustard

1 tablespoon white wine vinegar

3 tablespoons mayonnaise

¾ teaspoon honey

¼ cup buttermilk

2 to 4 (depending on size) heads Gem lettuce or 1 large head of Boston lettuce, leaves separated, washed, and dried (about 6 cups)

1 ripe avocado

Kosher salt and freshly ground black pepper

2 small tomatillos, husked, rinsed, and cut into small dice

3 tablespoons chopped red onion

3 tablespoons pumpkin seeds, toasted

4 tablespoons Tomatillo Salsa (recipe follows)

This one's all about the dressing—light but bracing, with just a touch of garlic. I've been known to drink any that's left over.

1. Make the dressing: Smash the garlic clove on a cutting board with a chef's knife and mash it into a paste with the salt. Transfer to a small bowl and whisk in the mustard, vinegar, mayonnaise, and honey. Gradually whisk in the buttermilk; the dressing should be creamy. Set aside.

2. Arrange the lettuce leaves on a large platter. Halve and pit the avocado and spoon out the flesh in bite-size pieces directly onto the lettuce. Drizzle the dressing over the lettuce and avocado. Season to taste with salt and pepper. Scatter the tomatillo, red onion, and pumpkin seeds over the top. Spoon small dollops of the tomatillo salsa here and there and serve immediately.

Continued

TOMATILLO SALSA

—

MAKES ABOUT 2 CUPS

1 pound tomatillos, husked, washed, and any stems pulled off

½ medium onion, quartered and root end trimmed

1 small jalapeño, halved and seeds removed if concerned about heat

Kosher salt and freshly ground black pepper

1. Preheat the oven to 400°F.

2. Place the tomatillos, onion, and jalapeño on a parchment- or foil-lined sheet pan and roast for about 25 minutes, until the tomatillos are soft and somewhat deflated and the onion and jalapeño are lightly browned. Let cool briefly.

3. Transfer the vegetables, along with any juices on the sheet pan, to the bowl of a food processor or to a blender and pulse, adding water 1 tablespoon at a time, until the salsa is a thick puree. Season to taste with salt and pepper.

MORE USES FOR TOMATILLO SALSA

• Stirred into chicken broth and served with tortilla chips and hot sauce for a lazy (wo)man's tortilla soup

• As an accompaniment to Six-Minute Eggs (page 72) or scrambled eggs

• Served with shrimp instead of classic cocktail sauce

Yellow Beets and Harissa Onions

—

SERVES 4

¼ cup flavorless
vegetable oil

1 teaspoon harissa,
plus more if desired

1 pound cipollini onions

1 pound small yellow beets,
ends trimmed

2 bay leaves

A few fresh thyme sprigs

1 garlic clove

4 large radicchio leaves,
cut crosswise into 1-inch
ribbons

Juice of 1 lemon, or to taste

Flaky salt and freshly
ground black pepper

⅓ cup small fresh dill sprigs

Spicy burnished onions contrast vividly with mild golden beets in this unusual dish, which is finished with a splash of lemon and fresh dill.

1. Pour the oil into a bowl large enough to hold the onions. Whisk in the harissa, taste, and add more if desired. Slice off the root and stem ends of the cipollini and remove any skin that comes off easily. Add the onions to the spiced oil, toss well, and let stand for at least 30 minutes, or overnight in the refrigerator.

2. Meanwhile, put the beets, bay leaves, thyme sprigs, and garlic in a large saucepan, add water to cover by several inches, and bring to a boil over high heat. Reduce the heat to a gentle boil and cook until the beets are tender enough to be pierced through with a fork, about 25 minutes; check early and often to avoid overcooking. Drain them in a colander, and when they are cool enough to handle, slip off the skins and cut them in half (or into quarters if they are large), so they are about the same size as the onions. Discard the herbs and garlic.

3. Preheat the oven to 400°F.

4. Arrange the onions on a sheet pan, spaced well apart, and roast for about 25 minutes, turning occasionally, until they are browned and tender and the remaining skin falls off. Transfer the onions to a cutting board; reserve the spiced oil remaining on the pan, and any bits of onion sticking to it.

5. Cut the onions in half and place in a serving bowl. Add the beets and most of the radicchio ribbons, reserving a few for garnish. Scrape the spiced oil and onion bits from the sheet pan onto the vegetables and toss well. Add the lemon juice and season with salt and pepper to taste. Shower with the dill and the reserved radicchio and serve.

Red

1 bunch of red beets
(about 1 pound), stems
and leaves removed
and reserved, root ends
trimmed

Pickling Liquid

½ cup sugar

½ cup red wine vinegar

A pinch of kosher salt

Kosher salt

1 cup red quinoa,
thoroughly rinsed and
drained

¾ cup Coriander Dressing
(page 33), plus more if
desired

1 cup shelled pistachios,
toasted

Freshly ground black
pepper

This strikingly red, many-textured salad of beets, pickled beet stems, and red quinoa is refreshing and satisfying. If your beets don't have much in the way of leaves, swap in some sliced red chard leaves and stems.

1. Separate the beet stems from the leaves, cut the stems into ½-inch pieces, and put in a small heatproof bowl; reserve the leaves. Grate the beets on the shredding disk of a food processor or coarse side of a box grater.

2. Make the pickling liquid: Combine the sugar, vinegar, and salt in a small saucepan and bring to a boil over medium heat. Boil gently, stirring occasionally, for a minute or two, until the sugar is dissolved. Pour over the cut stems and steep until cool. Use right away or store refrigerated in the brine in a tightly covered container for up to 2 weeks.

3. Drain the beet stems. You can reserve the pickling liquid, tightly covered in the refrigerator, for use as a shrub (a drinking vinegar) diluted with seltzer or in a cocktail within the next few days.

4. Bring a large pot of salted water to a boil. Add the quinoa and boil for 10 to 15 minutes, until the white germ ring is visible and the quinoa is tender but not mushy. Drain in a fine-mesh strainer and spread out on a sheet pan to cool. Break apart any clumps with your fingers.

5. Combine the grated beets, quinoa, and drained pickled beet stems in a large bowl. Add ½ cup of the dressing and toss to combine, fluffing up the quinoa as you go.

6. Just before serving, slice the beet leaves into ½-inch-wide ribbons. Add to the salad, along with the remaining ¼ cup dressing and the toasted pistachios, and toss well. Season to taste with salt and pepper, add more dressing if desired, and serve.

Continued

Stem Collection

Stop throwing out those thick stems! For an extra bite in a simple salad or a tangy condiment for a sandwich, pickle leftover stems with the pickling liquid on the previous page. If you are not sure if a particular stem will work (too woody? too bitter?), cut a few pieces into ¼-inch lengths and taste them.

Pickled red onions
(see page 174)

Diced chard
stems

Red chard
stems

Yellow and green
chard stems

Diced kale
stems

Diced yellow and green
chard stems

Carrot-Daikon Pickle
(page 48)

Pureed kale stems
with caraway seeds

Sourdough Bread Salad

—

SERVES 4

1½ cups cubed day-old sourdough bread

About 1 tablespoon extra-virgin olive oil

Walnut Dressing

1 teaspoon Dijon mustard

2 tablespoons sherry vinegar, or more to taste

1 shallot, minced

¼ cup extra-virgin olive oil

2 tablespoons walnut oil, or more to taste

A splash of walnut vinegar (optional)

1 large garlic clove, smashed

Kosher salt and freshly ground black pepper

4 large radicchio leaves, torn into bite-size pieces

A handful of frisée leaves, torn into large bite-size pieces

2 celery stalks, sliced on the diagonal (about ½ cup)

4 ounces Fontina, shaved into thin slices (see Quick Cut, page 85), then torn into bite-size pieces

⅓ cup walnuts, toasted and broken up

½ cup Roasted Grapes (page 152)

Every bite of this salad is a treat: crispy cubes of dressing-soaked sourdough bread, toasted walnuts, bitter greens, creamy Fontina cheese, celery, and roasted grapes that pop in your mouth.

1. Preheat the oven to 375°F.

2. Put the cubed bread on a sheet pan, drizzle lightly with olive oil, and spread out on the pan. Toast for about 7 minutes, until just starting to color. Transfer to a salad bowl.

3. Make the dressing: Whisk together the mustard, sherry vinegar, and minced shallot in a small bowl. Add the olive oil and walnut oil, along with the walnut vinegar, if desired, and mix together with a fork; do not try to emulsify the dressing. Spear the smashed garlic clove with the fork and mix up the dressing again to flavor it with the garlic. Season to taste with salt and pepper.

4. Pour half of the dressing over the bread cubes and toss, leaving the garlic in the remaining dressing. Let the bread soak in the dressing for about 20 minutes.

5. Just before serving, add the radicchio, frisée, celery, cheese, toasted walnuts, and roasted grapes and their juices (if any) to the bread. Remove any large pieces of garlic from the dressing and pour it over the salad, toss well, and season again, adding more walnut oil, sherry vinegar, and/or walnut vinegar if desired.

I Heart Fennel

—

SERVES 4

4 large fennel bulbs (about 2 pounds) with plenty of fresh fronds

6 tablespoons extra-virgin olive oil

Kosher salt

Grated zest of 1 lemon

2 tablespoons fresh lemon juice

2 tablespoons flavorless vegetable oil

Freshly ground black pepper

1 teaspoon fennel seeds, toasted

A pinch of fennel pollen (optional)

Consider this fragrant salad "nose-to-tail" fennel. Choose bulbs with the freshest, bushiest tops you can find. Fennel pollen is worth seeking out online for its elusive floral, almost curry-like fragrance.

1. Preheat the oven to 400°F.

2. Cut the fennel stalks from the bulbs and set aside. Trim the bottoms of the bulbs. With a sharp chef's knife, slice 3 of the bulbs lengthwise ⅓ inch to ½ inch thick. Trim out most of the tough core in a V-shape from the slices, leaving enough of it to hold the slices together. Set the fourth bulb aside.

3. Toss the sliced fennel with 3 tablespoons of the olive oil and salt to taste in a bowl, then arrange on a sheet pan, spacing the slices well apart. Roast for about 40 minutes, turning halfway through, or until tender and browned on both sides. Remove from the oven, and transfer the fennel to a bowl.

4. Meanwhile, pick about 1½ cups of the tender fronds from the reserved fennel stalks. Save the stalks to pickle (see Note, page 114) or use in a vegetable broth or soup. Put all but ⅓ cup of the fronds in the bowl of a food processor or in a blender and add the lemon zest and 1 tablespoon of the lemon juice. Pulse to finely chop and then, with the motor running, stream in 2 tablespoons of the olive oil and the vegetable oil, stopping to scrape down the sides as necessary; the dressing will be thick and green. Season to taste with salt and pepper. Add to the roasted fennel and toss gently until the slices are well coated.

5. Cut the remaining fennel bulb lengthwise in half and slice paper thin on a mandoline. Toss with the remaining 1 tablespoon each lemon juice and olive oil and season to taste with salt and pepper. Toss with the roasted fennel, then add the reserved fennel fronds, the seeds, and the pollen, if using, and toss again. Season to taste with salt and pepper and serve.

Bosc Pear and Fennel Slaw

—

SERVES 4

Lemon-Honey Dressing

3 tablespoons fresh lemon juice

½ teaspoon honey

6 tablespoons extra-virgin olive oil

2 small fennel bulbs

2 ripe but firm Bosc pears

Kosher salt

½ cup currants

½ cup sliced scallions

Cracked black pepper

This crisp, sweet, and tart slaw is a welcome counterpoint to traditional heavy cold-weather fare. Serve as a side salad or as a first course over mixed greens.

1. Make the dressing: Whisk the lemon juice and honey together in a small bowl. Gradually whisk in the olive oil until incorporated.

2. Trim the fennel. Cut the bulbs lengthwise in half and slice lengthwise on a mandoline as thin as possible. Place in a wide shallow bowl.

3. Cut the pears into quarters, remove the core, and slice lengthwise into sticks.

4. Add the pears to the fennel. Pour the dressing over them and toss thoroughly. Season to taste with salt. Add the currants and scallions. Toss again, sprinkle with pepper, and serve.

Maple-Miso Butternut Squash

SERVES 4 TO 6

1 medium butternut
squash (about 2½ pounds),
halved lengthwise, peeled,
seeded, and cut into
1½-inch cubes

3 tablespoons flavorless
vegetable oil

Kosher salt and freshly
ground black pepper

1 medium to large Asian
pear (8 to 12 ounces)

Maple-Miso Dressing
(recipe follows)

1 bunch of mustard greens
(about 3 cups), washed,
dried, trimmed, and torn
into bite-size pieces

½ cup soy nuts

Rich, deeply satisfying, salty, and sweet, this will
become a new classic at your Thanksgiving table.

1. Preheat the oven to 400°F.

2. Toss the cubed squash with the oil in a bowl and season
with salt and pepper to taste. Spread out on a sheet pan
and roast for about 20 minutes, until tender and lightly
browned. Remove from the oven and let cool completely.

3. Cut the pear into ¼-inch slices (follow the Quick Cut
instructions for slicing an apple on page 50). Combine
the pear with the roasted squash in a bowl and toss with
¾ cup of the dressing. Season to taste with salt and
pepper, and add more dressing if necessary to lightly
coat all the pieces of squash and pear.

4. Add the mustard greens to the salad, along with the soy
nuts. Toss and serve.

MAPLE-MISO DRESSING

MAKES ABOUT 1¼ CUPS

½ cup flavorless
vegetable oil

5½ tablespoons white
(shiro) miso

¼ cup maple syrup

2 tablespoons rice vinegar

1½ tablespoons water

Combine all the ingredients in the bowl of a food
processor or in a blender and process until well blended
and creamy. The dressing can be stored tightly covered in
the refrigerator for up to a week.

Palest Green

—

SERVES 4

2 tablespoons fresh
lemon juice

¼ cup extra-virgin olive oil

1 tart green apple, such
as Granny Smith (about
5 ounces)

A 5-ounce piece of daikon

Kosher salt and freshly
ground black pepper

One small chayote
(about 6 ounces)

A small handful of
sunflower greens and/or
microgreens (about
½ ounce)

The chayote and apples in this salad are both crisp and white with a hint of green. Leave the skin on both for the best effect. Sunflower greens and pretty microgreens, with flowers if you can find them, are available at the farmers' market or in small boxes at some supermarkets.

1. Whisk together the lemon juice and olive oil in a bowl large enough to hold the salad.

2. Slice the apple very thin (see Quick Cut, page 50). Immediately add to the bowl and toss with the dressing to prevent discoloration.

3. Peel the daikon and cut it into ¼-inch-thick slices. Stack the slices and cut into half-rounds. Add to the bowl, season the salad to taste with salt and pepper, and toss well.

4. Cut the chayote into quarters, cut the pit off at an angle, and cut the quarters into ¼-inch slices. Add to the bowl and toss again.

5. Spoon about one-third of the salad into a serving bowl. Scatter with some of the sunflower greens. Top with another layer of salad and more greens. Repeat, finishing with greens, and serve.

Roasted and Pickled Cauliflower

—

SERVES 4

1 medium head of cauliflower (about 2 pounds), cored and cut into medium florets (see Quick Cut, page 130), stems reserved

Pickling Liquid

½ cup cider vinegar

¼ cup sugar

A pinch of kosher salt

¼ cup extra-virgin olive oil, plus more if desired

Kosher salt and freshly ground black pepper

½ cup plain yogurt

⅔ cup walnuts, toasted and chopped

1 tablespoon nigella seeds or black sesame seeds

What began as a way of using leftover cauliflower (and floret crumbs) is now a favorite. Use any of the beautifully colored heads you find at the market. Serve this as a component of a meze platter or on a bed of peppery cress as a first course.

1. Preheat the oven to 400°F.

2. Cut enough of the smallest florets and pieces of stem into ½-inch pieces to make ⅓ cup for the pickled cauliflower. Place them in a small heatproof bowl. Combine the vinegar, sugar, and salt in a small saucepan and bring to a boil over medium heat. Boil gently, stirring occasionally, for a minute or two, until the sugar is dissolved. Pour the brine over the cauliflower and steep until cool. Use right away or store refrigerated in the brine for up to 2 weeks.

3. Toss the larger cauliflower florets with 2 tablespoons of the olive oil in a bowl and season to taste with salt and pepper. Arrange in one uncrowded layer on a large sheet pan. Roast for about 20 minutes, turning halfway through, until the cauliflower is nicely browned and crisped in parts. Let cool.

4. Transfer the roasted cauliflower to a serving bowl. Add the pickled cauliflower, the yogurt, the remaining 2 tablespoons olive oil, the walnuts, and two-thirds of the nigella seeds and toss to combine. Adjust the salt and pepper if necessary, sprinkle the remaining nigella seeds on top, and serve.

MEET THE INGREDIENT

Nigella Seeds

Nigella seeds, known as kalonji in India, often go by the misnomer "black onion seeds" in the United States, but the two are not related. Dark, teardrop-shaped nigella seeds have a deep, slightly exotic flavor that is altogether unique. Buy them at spice markets or online at Kalustyans.com.

Not-Exactly-Manchurian Cauliflower

—

SERVES 4

1 head of cauliflower, cut into medium florets, core reserved and tender part sliced, leaves left whole (see Quick Cut on the following page)

One 6-ounce can tomato paste

2 teaspoons molasses

2 teaspoons cumin seeds, toasted and ground

Kosher salt and freshly ground black pepper

¼ cup flavorless vegetable oil

⅓ cup minced jalapeño

⅓ cup finely minced fresh ginger

1 large garlic clove, finely minced

4 or 5 scallions, thinly sliced on the diagonal

1 tablespoon extra-virgin olive oil

Flaky salt

This is a simplified and not-fried version of Gobi Manchurian, an Indian restaurant favorite of fried cauliflower seasoned Indo-Chinese style. Try to find a head of cauliflower that still has its leaves.

1. Preheat the oven to 400°F.

2. Bring a large pot of water to a boil. Add the cauliflower florets, return to a boil, and cook for about 1 minute, until the florets are just tender. Drain thoroughly and transfer to a sheet pan to cool.

3. Whisk together the tomato paste, molasses, cumin seeds, 1 teaspoon kosher salt, ¼ teaspoon pepper, and 3 tablespoons of the oil in a small bowl until thoroughly blended.

4. Heat the remaining tablespoon of oil in a small skillet over medium heat and sauté the jalapeño, ginger, and garlic for a minute or two, until soft and fragrant but not browned. Season to taste with kosher salt and pepper and add to the tomato mixture, whisking to thoroughly combine.

5. Put the cauliflower florets in a large bowl and toss with the tomato mixture, rubbing the mixture into the florets' cracks and crevices. Taste and add more kosher salt if necessary. Spread out on the same sheet pan and roast for 15 minutes. Rotate the pan and roast for 10 minutes more, or until the florets are tender and browned, even charred in some spots. Meanwhile, toss the slices of core and the leaves with oil and kosher salt and pepper to taste. Roast on a separate small pan just until browned, about 7 minutes. Let the florets, core slices, and leaves cool.

6. Transfer the cauliflower florets, leaves, and slices of core to a bowl, add most of the scallions, and toss to combine. Transfer to a platter, drizzle with the olive oil, and scatter the reserved scallions and some flaky salt over the top. Serve.

Continued

Breaking Down a Head of Cauliflower

A cool trick for fast florets.

1 Set the cauliflower upside down on a cutting board. Using a sharp paring knife, cut all the way around the core at the base of the florets, releasing them onto the board as you go. You may need to do this in two passes.

2 Trim or break the larger florets so that the pieces are evenly sized. Trim away the tough parts of the core, but reserve the tender parts and nice-looking leaves, which can be blanched and roasted, too.

Toasty Broccoli with Curry Leaves and Coconut

—

SERVES 4

½ cup flavorless
vegetable oil

½ ounce curry leaves,
preferably fresh, long
stems removed

½ cup unsweetened dried
coconut chips

Kosher salt

1 large bunch of broccoli,
cut into florets with 2 to
3 inches of stem attached

Try this dish and your kitchen will be filled with the intoxicating aromas of Southeast Asia.

1. Preheat the oven to 425°F.

2. Meanwhile, line a plate with paper towels for draining the curry leaves and coconut chips. Heat the oil in a medium skillet over medium-high heat until it shimmers. Add the curry leaves and fry, turning occasionally with a skimmer, for a minute or two, until crisp and shiny (dried leaves will crisp faster). Transfer to the paper towels. Fry the coconut chips, stirring constantly, for 10 to 15 seconds, just until they are an even golden brown, then spread them out on the paper towels to drain and sprinkle with salt. Reserve the oil to coat the broccoli. (The curry leaves and coconut chips can be fried a day ahead and stored between layers of paper towels in an airtight container. Store the oil in a covered container in the refrigerator.)

3. Bring a large pot of water to a rolling boil over high heat and set a colander in the sink. Add the broccoli florets to the boiling water and cook for a minute or two, until the florets turn a more vivid green but retain their crispness. Drain them in the colander and pat very dry.

4. Put the broccoli florets on a sheet pan, toss with 2 tablespoons of the reserved frying oil and salt to taste, and spread out on the pan. Roast for 20 to 25 minutes, until crisp and browned in parts. Put the broccoli in a bowl, add the curry leaves and coconut chips, reserving a few curry leaves and a tablespoon of the coconut chips for garnish, and toss together. Season to taste with salt. Heap the broccoli on a platter, scatter the reserved curry leaves and coconut over the top, and serve.

Continued

Curry Leaves

The leaves of the curry tree, unrelated to the spice mix, have an exotic herbalness unlike that of anything else. If you're not familiar with them, you should be—soon you'll be adding them to soups and stocks, infusing them into an oil, even steeping the fresh leaves in hot water as a tisane. Look for the fresh leaves at Indian grocers and online at Kalustyans.com. They will keep, tightly wrapped, for a month or more in the freezer.

Roots and Leaves

—

SERVES 4

2 small beets, one yellow, one Chioggia (aka candy-striped), trimmed and scrubbed

4 small radishes or 1 larger radish (such as watermelon), trimmed and scrubbed

6 small white Japanese or scarlet turnips, trimmed and scrubbed

2 purple carrots, trimmed and scrubbed

3 ounces greens, such as mustard, bok choy, purslane, sorrel, radicchio, and small head lettuces

¼ cup extra-virgin olive oil, or more to taste

2 tablespoons sherry vinegar, or more to taste

Kosher salt and freshly ground black pepper

½ cup pickled red onions (see page 174)

Late fall and winter salads can be a study in color and geometry. Choose multihued radishes and carrots and scarlet or sweet white salad turnips, and, if you like, experiment to find their most interesting cuts. To complete the collage, add beautiful lettuces and leaves in greens, yellows, and purples.

1. Thinly slice the beets, radishes, and turnips on a mandoline. Halve if large. Set aside in a small bowl of ice water. Thinly slice the carrots lengthwise on the mandoline and put in the bowl of ice water.

2. Put the greens in a medium bowl and dress with 2 tablespoons of the olive oil and 1 tablespoon of the sherry vinegar. Season to taste with salt and pepper, and add more oil and/or vinegar if desired.

3. Drain the carrots and beets and pat thoroughly dry. Put the turnips and radishes in a medium bowl, add the carrots and beets, and dress with the remaining 2 tablespoons olive oil and 1 tablespoon sherry vinegar. Season to taste with salt and pepper and add more oil and/or vinegar if desired.

4. Combine the greens, pickled red onions, and vegetables in a wide shallow serving bowl and toss together very lightly. Look for especially beautiful slices of vegetables and leaves and pull them up toward the top so they can be seen. Serve.

Curling and Crisping Vegetables with Ice Water

Thinly shaved carrots, beets, and kohlrabi—and scallions sliced lengthwise—will stay crisp and curl attractively for a sculptural garnish if held in a bowl of ice water until ready to serve.

Beans and Sprouts, Bacon and Sorrel

—

SERVES 8

1 pound dried cranberry beans (borlotti), soaked in water to cover for at least 6 hours, or overnight

3 garlic cloves

2 bay leaves

1 teaspoon black peppercorns

Kosher salt

8 ounces slab bacon, pancetta, or thick-cut sliced bacon

2 ounces red, green, or French sorrel, or substitute arugula

6 ounces crunchy mixed bean sprouts, rinsed and dried

6 tablespoons extra-virgin olive oil, plus more for drizzling

Freshly ground black pepper

Velvety and crunchy, smoky and lemony.

1. Drain the soaked beans and put them in a large pot, along with the garlic, bay leaves, black peppercorns, and cold water to cover by several inches. Bring to a boil and skim off the foam, then reduce the heat to a gentle boil and cook for about an hour, until the beans are tender but not mushy; salt the water toward the end of the cooking time. Drain, reserving the bean broth for a future soup if desired. Discard the bay leaves, garlic, and peppercorns.

2. Meanwhile, cut the slab bacon or pancetta into ½-inch-thick lardons, or cut the sliced bacon into 1-inch-wide strips. Put in a cold skillet set over medium-low heat and cook, turning occasionally, until most of the fat is rendered and the bacon is almost crisp, about 10 minutes. Drain on paper towels, reserving the fat.

3. Wash and dry the sorrel. If the leaves are large, tear them into smaller pieces and chop the stems; if they are small, leave them whole.

4. Put the beans and bean sprouts in a large bowl. Add the olive oil and salt and pepper to taste and toss gently to combine, taking care not to break the beans. Add the bacon and 3 tablespoons of the reserved bacon fat and toss again.

5. Spoon about one-third of the bean salad into a serving bowl. Scatter one-third of the sorrel over it, and repeat twice more, finishing with sorrel. Drizzle with additional olive oil. Serve.

Sweet Potatoes and Chickpeas, Bhel Puri Style

SERVES 8

2¼ pounds sweet potatoes, scrubbed and cut into 1-inch pieces

3 tablespoons flavorless vegetable oil

Kosher salt

1 cup shredded unsweetened coconut

Tamarind Dressing

1 tablespoon Dijon mustard

3 tablespoons rice vinegar

½ cup tamarind concentrate

½ cup flavorless vegetable oil

Kosher salt

2 cups cooked or canned drained chickpeas

¼ cup chopped fresh mint leaves

¼ cup small fresh cilantro sprigs

Freshly ground black pepper

¾ cup plus 2 tablespoons Bhel mix, or other Indian snack mix

Lime wedges

Fresh Green Chutney (recipe follows)

Inspired by a craving for Bhel Puri, my favorite Indian street food, I decided to make a salad with some of its key components: tamarind dressing, onion, mint, and cilantro—and, of course, Bhel mix.

1. Preheat the oven to 400°F.

2. Toss the sweet potatoes with the oil and spread out on a sheet pan. Sprinkle with salt and roast for about 20 minutes, turning occasionally, until nicely browned outside and tender inside.

3. Spread the coconut out on a second sheet pan and toast in the oven for about 5 minutes, until fragrant and lightly colored, stirring halfway through. Set aside.

4. Make the dressing: Put the mustard, rice vinegar, and tamarind liquid in the bowl of a food processor or in a blender and pulse to combine. With the motor running, drizzle in the oil. The mixture will be creamy. Add salt to taste.

5. Transfer the sweet potatoes to a serving bowl and toss with the chickpeas, herbs, and dressing. Season generously with salt and pepper. Let cool to room temperature. Just before serving, add the coconut and ¾ cup of the Bhel mix to the sweet potatoes and toss to combine. Top with the remaining 2 tablespoons of Bhel mix and serve with lime wedges and the chutney.

Continued

| MEET THE INGREDIENT |

Bhel Mix

Most Indian grocers sell packaged snack mixes (like Bhel mix) made up of lentils, chickpeas, puffed rice, fried onions, noodles, and spices. Some are hot, some are mild, all are addictive. If you don't have an Indian market near you, look for them online.

FRESH GREEN CHUTNEY

—

MAKES ABOUT 1 CUP

¾ cup chopped white or yellow onion

¼ cup finely chopped fresh mint leaves

¼ cup finely chopped fresh cilantro leaves

1 tablespoon minced jalapeño pepper

Juice of 1 lime or lemon

Kosher salt and freshly ground pepper

Just the thing to contrast with the mellow and nutty flavor of this dish, the chutney adds a tart, spicy zip.

Combine all the ingredients in a small bowl and mix well. Season to taste with salt and pepper. Refrigerate until ready to serve (best eaten the same day).

MORE USES FOR FRESH GREEN CHUTNEY

• Swirled into a bean soup

• Tossed with sliced cucumbers and radishes, olive oil, and additional salt and pepper

• As a garnish for sautéed greens such as spinach

Farro with Five Jewels

—

SERVES 6 TO 8

Kosher salt

1½ cups farro

3 tablespoons extra-virgin olive oil, plus more for drizzling

1 large sweet potato, peeled and cut into small dice (about ¼ inch)

½ small onion, chopped

A 1½-inch knob of ginger, peeled and minced

⅓ cup Pickled Raisins (recipe follows), plus a little extra brine

¼ cup chopped dried apricots

¼ cup diced prunes

⅓ cup whole, unblanched almonds, toasted and roughly chopped

1 or 2 Fresno or other medium-hot red chiles, minced (to taste)

½ cup fresh flat-leaf parsley

Freshly ground black pepper

This sweet and savory grain dish is inspired by tzimmes, the Ashkenazi Jewish stew of carrots and dried fruit. Here, farro is embellished with glistening bits of sweet potato, apricots, and prunes, pickled raisins, and the fruity heat of Fresno chiles. Serve it alongside roast chicken, or use it as stuffing for your holiday turkey.

1. Bring a large pot of salted water to a boil. Add the farro, return to a boil, and cook for 15 to 20 minutes, until tender but not soft. Drain and spread out on a sheet pan to cool.

2. When the farro is cool, drizzle with 1 tablespoon of the olive oil and toss gently.

3. Heat 1 tablespoon of the olive oil in a large skillet over medium-low heat. Add the sweet potato, onion, and ginger and sauté for several minutes until the sweet potato is tender. If the onion starts to brown too quickly, add a tablespoon of water, stir, and cover the pan. When the sweet potato is tender, remove from the heat and let cool.

4. Put the pickled raisins in a small bowl with the chopped apricots and prunes. Mix together with your fingers to separate and coat all in the brine.

5. Put the farro in a wide bowl and fluff with a fork. Add the dried fruit, almonds, chile, and parsley. Toss with the remaining tablespoon of olive oil and a bit more of the raisin pickling liquid. Season to taste with salt and pepper, drizzle with additional olive oil to taste, toss again, and serve.

Continued

PICKLED RAISINS

—

MAKES ABOUT 2 CUPS

One 8-ounce box raisins

1 cup white wine vinegar

⅓ cup sugar

1½ teaspoons coriander seeds

1½ teaspoons cumin seeds

1 bay leaf

A pinch of kosher salt

½ small onion, finely chopped

1. Put the raisins in a small heatproof bowl.

2. Combine the white wine vinegar, sugar, coriander seeds, cumin seeds, bay leaf, salt, and onion in a small saucepan and bring to a boil over medium heat. Boil gently, stirring occasionally, for a minute or two, until the sugar is completely dissolved.

3. Pour the brine over the raisins. Refrigerate overnight before using. The pickled raisins will keep for 2 weeks or more tightly covered in the refrigerator.

MORE USES FOR PICKLED RAISINS

• To spice up a carrot salad

• To add unexpected dimension to a classic bread pudding or rice pudding

• As a garnish for a beet and goat cheese salad with rye croutons and Caraway Dressing (page 167)

• As an addition to an Indian curry

• As a sweet counterpoint for a charcuterie/salumi platter

Choose-Your-Style Brussels Sprouts

—

SERVES 4

Kosher salt

1½ pounds Brussels sprouts of similar size

2 tablespoons flavorless vegetable oil

Freshly ground black pepper

Extra-virgin olive oil for drizzling

To bring out the best in Brussels sprouts, blanch them first to keep them moist and roast them to caramelize. Then take them on one of the flavor journeys opposite!

START HERE

1. Preheat the oven to 425°F. Bring a large pot of salted water to a rolling boil over high heat.

2. Trim the bottoms of the sprouts and discard any shriveled leaves. Cut a small X in the bottom of each sprout with a paring knife.

3. Add the sprouts to the boiling water. When they are bright green but still crisp, after about 4 minutes, depending on size, drain well and blot dry.

4. If your sprouts are large, cut them in half.

5. Toss the sprouts with the vegetable oil on a sheet pan, add salt and pepper to taste, and arrange in a single layer on the pan. Roast until deeply caramelized, about 30 minutes, shaking the pan halfway through to turn the sprouts over. Season with a bit more salt and pepper if necessary and add olive oil to taste. Then choose your style from the chart opposite, toss, and serve.

NOW YOU KNOW

Charring Brussels Sprouts Leaves

If you trim the larger sprouts deeply, you will get a quantity of nice extra leaves. Oven-char them separately and add to a grain salad (see page 149) or toss with any of the styles opposite for textural variety. Or simply sprinkle with salt and snack on them.

CHOOSE YOUR STYLE

YANKEE	KASBAH	MIDEAST	TEX-MEX

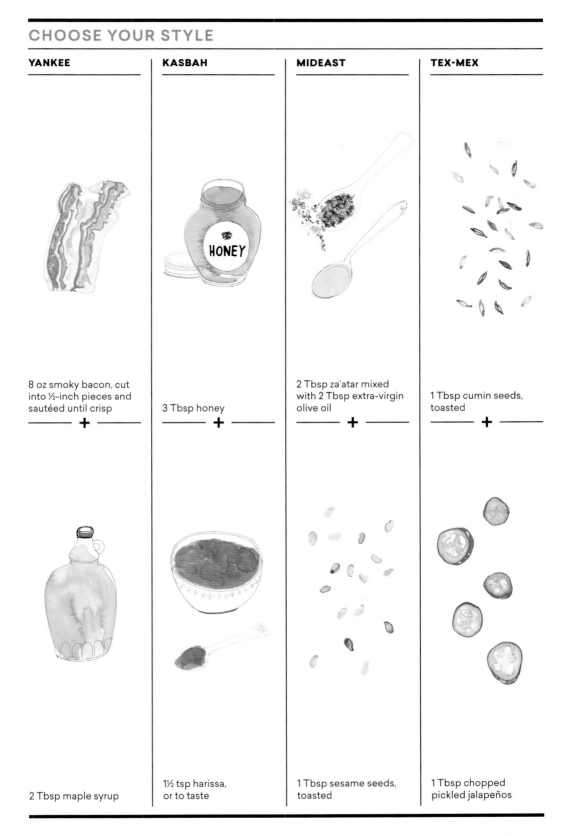

YANKEE

8 oz smoky bacon, cut into ½-inch pieces and sautéed until crisp

+

2 Tbsp maple syrup

KASBAH

3 Tbsp honey

+

1½ tsp harissa, or to taste

MIDEAST

2 Tbsp za'atar mixed with 2 Tbsp extra-virgin olive oil

+

1 Tbsp sesame seeds, toasted

TEX-MEX

1 Tbsp cumin seeds, toasted

+

1 Tbsp chopped pickled jalapeños

Barley with Many Mushrooms

—

SERVES 4 TO 6

Kosher salt

1 cup pearled barley

½ cup extra-virgin olive oil, plus more if needed

Freshly ground black pepper

1½ cups Brussels sprouts leaves, or shaved whole Brussels sprouts

1 large onion, chopped

2 pounds mixed cremini, shiitake, oyster, or other mushrooms, cleaned, trimmed, and cut into evenly sized pieces

1 tablespoon fresh thyme leaves

1 cup walnuts, toasted and roughly chopped

3 large stalks celery, sliced diagonally ¼ inch thick

Super-hearty and satisfying, this dish is truly a meal by itself. A mix of oyster, shiitake, and cremini mushrooms adds complexity, and oven-charred Brussels sprouts make it complete.

1. Preheat the oven to 400°F.

2. Bring a large pot of salted water to a boil. Add the barley and cook until tender but still chewy, about 30 minutes. Drain thoroughly in a colander, and spread out on a baking sheet to cool. Drizzle lightly with a tablespoon of olive oil and season to taste with salt and pepper. Fluff up the grains with a fork to separate them. When the barley is cool, transfer it to a large bowl.

3. Meanwhile, scatter the Brussels sprouts leaves over a sheet pan. Drizzle and toss with a tablespoon of olive oil, sprinkle with salt, and roast for about 5 minutes, until the edges are lightly charred. Set aside to cool. Some will be more done than others, and that's fine.

4. Add 2 tablespoons of oil to a large skillet over low heat, and sauté the onions until tender and very lightly browned. Remove with a slotted spoon, leaving the onion-flavored oil in the skillet, and add to the barley.

5. Add 2 tablespoons of fresh olive oil to what's left in the skillet and raise the heat to medium-high. Add as many mushrooms as will fit in one layer comfortably without crowding, sprinkle with thyme, and sauté, tossing occasionally, for several minutes, until nicely browned and crisp on all sides. Transfer to a large serving bowl and repeat with the remaining mushrooms, adding more oil if necessary. Season to taste with salt and pepper. Add to the barley and onions, scraping in any remaining oil and other bits in the pan. Add the walnuts and celery, then the Brussels sprouts leaves. Season again to taste with salt and pepper and serve.

Red Potatoes with Chorizo and Roasted Grapes

—

1 pound small red potatoes, scrubbed and halved or quartered, depending on size

1 small onion, cut into pieces the same size as the potatoes

2 tablespoons extra-virgin olive oil

½ teaspoon pimentón dulce de la Vera

Kosher salt and freshly ground black pepper

12 ounces soft, Spanish-style, fully cooked chorizo sausage

Roasted Grapes (recipe follows)

2 tablespoons capers

½ cup fresh flat-leaf parsley

A solid meat-and-potatoes dish—with a surprise ending of sweet roasted grapes.

1. Preheat the oven to 400°F.

2. Put the potatoes and onions on a sheet pan and toss with the olive oil. Sprinkle with the pimentón and salt and pepper to taste and toss again. Spread out on the pan and roast for about 20 minutes, turning occasionally, until the potatoes are tender and nicely browned. If the onions are browning more quickly than the potatoes, remove them before they burn and transfer them to a plate.

3. Meanwhile, cut the chorizo lengthwise in half, then cut on the bias into ½-inch slices. Put the chorizo in a small skillet set over medium-low heat and cook, turning occasionally, until browned on all sides and heated through.

4. Put the chorizo in a serving bowl, add the potatoes, onions, and roasted grapes with their juices (if any), and toss lightly together, taking care not to break up the potatoes. Toss in most of the capers and parsley, scatter the remainder over the top, and serve.

Continued

ROASTED GRAPES

—

MAKES ABOUT 1 CUP

8 ounces small red
seedless grapes

1. Preheat the oven to 400°F.

2. Remove the stems from the grapes and spread the grapes out on a sheet pan. Roast for 10 to 12 minutes, until shiny, somewhat softened, slightly browned, and releasing some liquid, shaking the pan occasionally if they start to stick.

3. Using a spatula, carefully transfer the grapes and their juices to a plate to cool before using.

MORE USES FOR ROASTED GRAPES

- Combined with crisp-cooked diced pancetta and thyme as a garnish for lentil soup

- As an addition to Thanksgiving bread stuffing

- As a topping for crackers spread with fromage blanc to make an upscale "cream cheese and jelly sandwich" hors d'oeuvre

- Added to a salad of wilted romaine hearts and crumbled blue cheese dressed with olive oil

A "Dinner of No" Menu

There's no meat, no dairy, and no gluten here, but this healthy, colorful, and festive menu hits all the right notes for a satisfying dinner in the fall, or any season for that matter. The Coriander Dressing called for in Red does double duty, with a few tablespoons reserved for the "Peas and Carrots" on Papadum. It tastes completely different in each dish. Double, triple, or quadruple recipes as necessary to feed your crowd.

——

MAKE THIS:

"Peas and Carrots" on Papadum (page 33)

Red (page 113)

I Heart Fennel (page 119)

Maple-Miso Butternut Squash (page 123)

Toasty Broccoli with Curry Leaves and Coconut (page 131)

ADD THIS:

Dried Fruit Compote (opposite) served over or alongside vegan ice cream

Pink Peppered Potato Vodka Shots with Petals (opposite)

BUY THIS:

Raw chocolate, broken into chunks

Kombucha

Dried Fruit Compote

—

MAKES ABOUT 2 CUPS

Put 3 cups mixed dried fruit, such as figs, pitted dates, dried cherries or cranberries, apricots, prunes, or raisins (larger fruit halved or quartered), in a saucepan and add 1½ cups apple cider and 2 tablespoons apple cider vinegar. Bring to a boil over medium heat and cook for about 10 minutes, until the fruit is soft and plump and the liquid is syrupy.

Remove from the heat and add the zest of 1 small orange, 2 tablespoons orange juice, and freshly ground black pepper to taste. Serve warm or at room temperature with ice cream, and scatter chopped salted almonds over the top if desired. The compote can be stored, covered, in the refrigerator for up to 2 weeks.

Pink Peppered Potato Vodka Shots with Petals

—

SERVES 8

With the bottom of a small heavy skillet, lightly crush 24 to 32 pink peppercorns (to taste) on a cutting board. Divide among 8 shot glasses.

Fill each glass with 1½ ounces of iced potato vodka (preferably Tito's) and float one or two nasturtium petals on top of each shot. Serve immediately.

Satisfying
Sustenance

WINTER

Stock up and hunker down with cabbages and kale. Add grains and beans, and don't forget all those interesting condiments you've collected in your pantry.

———

Cold-Weather Crudités with Seeded Yogurt Dip

—

Seeded Yogurt Dip

1 tablespoon white sesame seeds

1 tablespoon coriander seeds

1 tablespoon fennel seeds

1½ teaspoons caraway seeds

½ teaspoon black sesame seeds

3 cups plain yogurt

Kosher salt and freshly ground black pepper

6 tablespoons extra-virgin olive oil

3 to 4 pounds vegetables, including broccoli, cauliflower, and/or Romanesco, separated into florets; beets, white Japanese turnips, and/or small kohlrabi, scrubbed and trimmed; and medium carrots, trimmed

1 large Granny Smith apple, cored and cut into thick wedges

6 tablespoons extra-virgin olive oil

Kosher salt and freshly ground black pepper

Oven-charred winter vegetables and fruit, slightly softened but still a bit crunchy, make a welcome change from cut-up raw vegetables when there's a chill in the air. You'll need about ¾ pound untrimmed produce per person.

1. Make the yogurt dip: Toast all the seeds together in a dry skillet over medium heat for a minute or two, tossing occasionally, until fragrant; do not allow them to burn. Remove from the heat.

2. Put the yogurt in a serving bowl and add the toasted seeds. Season to taste with salt and pepper. Whisk in the olive oil and let sit for about 30 minutes to allow the flavors to blend, then refrigerate, covered with plastic wrap, until ready to serve.

3. Preheat the oven to 425°F.

4. Arrange the broccoli, cauliflower, Romanesco, and apple on a sheet pan and toss with 3 tablespoons of the olive oil. Season to taste with salt and pepper. Cut the beets, turnips, carrots, and kohlrabi lengthwise in half, or into quarters if large. Spread them out on a second sheet pan, drizzle with the remaining 3 tablespoons olive oil, and toss to coat. If using red beets, place them on a piece of foil, with the edges folded up to form a rim, to keep their juices from staining the other root vegetables. Season to taste with salt and pepper.

5. Roast the broccoli, cauliflower, Romanesco, and apple for 10 to 15 minutes, turning them halfway through. Roast the root vegetables for 15 to 20 minutes, turning them halfway through. The vegetables (and apple) should be slightly softened but still crisp and browned in spots. Let cool to room temperature.

6. Arrange the vegetables in groups on a serving platter or board. Serve with the chilled yogurt dip on the side.

Slightly Spicy Carrots with Buckwheat Honey

SERVES 4

1 pound good-size carrots, trimmed and peeled

2 tablespoons extra-virgin olive oil

2 tablespoons buckwheat honey

1 tablespoon boiling water

1 bunch of chives, cut into 1-inch lengths

Grated zest and juice of 1 lemon

½ cup salted dry-roasted peanuts

Kosher salt and freshly ground black pepper

Shichimi togarashi (see page 17)

This dish is a wonderful introduction to a favorite and versatile spice blend: Japanese shichimi togarashi, a mix that includes chile flakes, sesame seeds, and dried orange or tangerine zest. A little jar comes with me wherever I go.

1. Bring a large pot of water to a boil. Meanwhile, cut the carrots into 1- to 1½-inch-long wedges (see Quick Cut on the following page). Add the carrots to the boiling water and cook for about 5 minutes, until tender but not soft. Drain and place in a bowl.

2. Pour the olive oil over the carrots, then add the honey and the 1 tablespoon boiling water and toss to combine. Toss in the chives, lemon zest and juice, and peanuts. Season with salt and pepper and togarashi to taste, toss to combine, and serve.

Continued

MEET THE INGREDIENT

Buckwheat Honey

Buckwheat honey is dark and rich, with a distinct savory flavor—an interesting contrast to lighter honeys. It's intense, so a little goes a long way. Try it in your morning yogurt with granola or even on pancakes; it's also great with pork.

Roll-Cutting Carrots

To get polished-looking wedge-shaped pieces out of a plain old fat carrot:

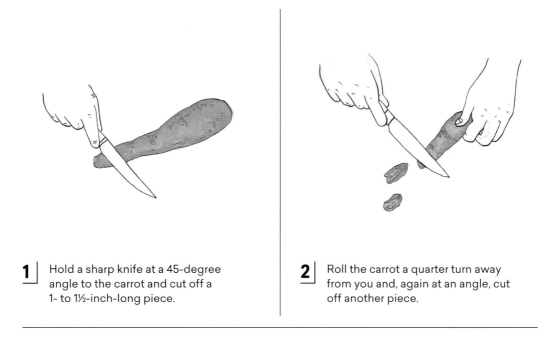

1 | Hold a sharp knife at a 45-degree angle to the carrot and cut off a 1- to 1½-inch-long piece.

2 | Roll the carrot a quarter turn away from you and, again at an angle, cut off another piece.

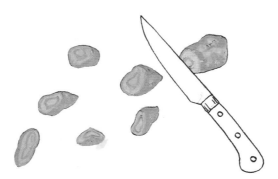

3 | Continue in this fashion until you reach the end of the carrot.

Broccoli Rabe with Roasted Oyster Mushrooms

—

SERVES 4

1 pound oyster mushrooms

1 tablespoon fresh
thyme leaves

¾ cup extra-virgin olive oil

3 large garlic cloves,
finely chopped

½ teaspoon chile flakes

3 anchovy fillets packed
in olive oil, drained and
roughly chopped

Kosher salt and freshly
ground black pepper

1 bunch of broccoli rabe,
thick stems removed,
rinsed, and excess water
shaken off

1 large lemon, halved

Oyster mushrooms soak up the classic Italian flavors here like little sponges. The anchovies add depth, and they virtually disappear when sautéed.

1. Preheat the oven to 400°F.

2. Line two sheet pans with parchment paper. Cut the center cores out of the mushroom clusters and separate the mushrooms into "petals." Scatter them evenly over one lined pan and sprinkle with the thyme leaves. Roast the mushrooms for about 8 minutes, or until browned in parts, crisp, and somewhat dry. Transfer to a bowl.

3. Meanwhile, pour the olive oil into a small skillet set over medium-low heat, add the garlic, chile flakes, and anchovies, and sauté until the oil starts to bubble and the garlic just starts to lightly color. Immediately remove the pan from the heat and pour the contents into a small heatproof bowl. Spoon 6 tablespoons of the mixture over the warm mushrooms, toss to coat, and season to taste with salt and pepper.

Continued

MORE USES FOR ROASTED OYSTER MUSHROOMS

- Scattered over warm polenta, along with shaved Parmesan and toasted pine nuts

- As a topping for your favorite melted cheese on toast

- As a cocktail snack on toothpicks, or alongside jarred or homemade pickled vegetables, olives, and spiced nuts

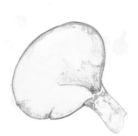

4. Arrange the broccoli rabe on the second lined sheet pan, stems facing outward. Spoon the remaining 6 tablespoons anchovy-garlic oil over it and roast for about 5 minutes, until the broccoli is wilted but still bright green. The greens will get a little crispy in the oven.

5. Arrange the broccoli rabe alongside the roasted mushrooms on a serving platter, squeeze the juice of the lemon over the top, and serve.

NOW YOU KNOW

Oven-Blanching

Most sturdy greens can be lightly oiled and salted, then briefly "blanched" on a sheet pan in a 400°F oven. The dry heat of the hot oven crisps and wilts them at the same time, providing a broader range of textures than the usual parboil or sauté.

Cabbage and
Kraut

Cabbage and
Kimchi

Cabbage and Kraut

—

SERVES 4

Caraway Dressing

2 teaspoons caraway seeds

2 tablespoons cider vinegar

1½ teaspoons honey

¼ cup flavorless vegetable oil

Kosher salt and freshly ground black pepper

1 cup sauerkraut

3 cups thinly sliced Savoy or other green cabbage

½ unpeeled small red apple

3 tablespoons pecans, toasted and coarsely chopped

Scant ¼ cup raisins

Kosher salt and freshly ground black pepper

Cabbage two ways—raw and fermented—is a study in contrasts: mild and punchy, crunchy and tender.

1. Make the dressing: Combine the caraway seeds, vinegar, and honey in the bowl of a food processor or in a blender and pulse to combine. With the motor running, slowly drizzle in the oil and process until the mixture is emulsified. Season to taste with salt and pepper. The dressing keeps for about 5 days in a covered container in the fridge.

2. Drain the sauerkraut in a colander, pressing down to remove excess liquid. Turn it out into a large bowl and add the cabbage. Add the dressing and thoroughly mix the ingredients together, rubbing the sauerkraut into the cabbage with your fingers.

3. Cut the apple into ¼-inch-thick slices (see Quick Cut, page 50). Add the apples to the dressed cabbage, along with the pecans and the raisins. Toss again, season to taste with salt and pepper, and serve.

VARIATION

Cabbage and Kimchi

Substitute 1 cup red kimchi for the sauerkraut. Drain the kimchi, reserving the liquid, and chop. Use half an Asian pear instead of the apple. Omit the pecans. Instead of the caraway dressing, whisk 2 or 3 tablespoons of the kimchi liquid with a few drops of toasted sesame oil and a teaspoon of toasted black sesame seeds. Use goji berries instead of raisins.

Red Cabbage and Chickpeas with a Kick

SERVES 4

3 large scallions

2 cups cooked or canned drained chickpeas

12 ounces red cabbage, trimmed of outer leaves, cored, and thinly sliced (about 4 cups)

¾ cup Spicy Tahini Dressing (recipe follows)

1 tablespoon white sesame seeds, toasted

2 tablespoons fresh lemon juice

Kosher salt and freshly ground black pepper

1 lemon, cut into wedges, for garnish

This earthy slaw gets its heat from a harissa-spiked tahini dressing, which makes more than you need for this recipe. It's addictive as a dip for raw vegetables, or spooned alongside roasted ones.

1. Trim the scallions and slice them about ¼ inch thick, cutting the white parts straight across and the green parts on the diagonal; keep them separate.

2. Pour the chickpeas into a large bowl. Add the cabbage and the white parts of the scallions and toss to combine. Add the dressing, sesame seeds, and lemon juice and mix thoroughly. Season to taste with salt and pepper. Transfer to a serving bowl and scatter the scallion greens on top. Garnish with the lemon wedges.

SPICY TAHINI DRESSING

—

MAKES 1¼ CUPS

1 cup roasted tahini (stir well before measuring), at room temperature

Grated zest and juice of 1 lemon

1 small garlic clove (optional)

¾ cup water

1 teaspoon harissa, or to taste (brands vary in concentration and spiciness)

¼ teaspoon kosher salt, or to taste

Combine the tahini, lemon zest and juice, garlic, if using, and water in the bowl of a food processor or in a blender and process to combine. Check the consistency—it should be thin enough to toss with the cabbage; add another tablespoon or two of water if needed. Add the harissa and salt and process until smooth. The dressing keeps for several days in a covered container in the refrigerator.

MEET THE INGREDIENT

Tahini

Tahini, otherwise known as sesame paste, is available in any supermarket, but for something special, look for an artisanal tahini such as Seed + Mill. The consistency varies from brand to brand, but any tahini tends to separate and needs to be stirred before measuring. Once opened, it should be stored in the refrigerator.

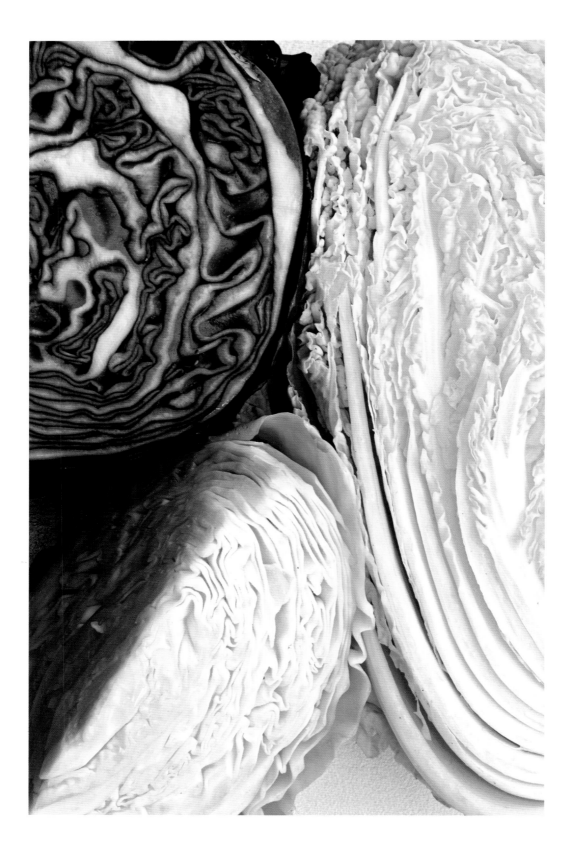

Sunchoke and Endive Slaw

—

SERVES 4

2 tablespoons fresh
lemon juice

¼ cup extra-virgin olive oil

8 ounces sunchokes,
scrubbed well and trimmed
of dark spots

2 large endives

6 pitted dates, cut
lengthwise into slivers

½ cup shelled pistachios,
toasted and coarsely
chopped

1 tablespoon capers

Kosher salt and freshly
ground black pepper

Fresh lemon juice, sweet dates, and salty capers
enliven this light, crisp slaw.

1. Whisk together the lemon juice and olive oil in a bowl
large enough to hold the rest of the ingredients.

2. Slice the sunchokes about ¼ inch thick, then stack the
slices and cut into matchsticks about ¼ inch thick. Add to
the lemon dressing and toss well to prevent discoloration.

3. Trim the root ends off the endives and slice them
lengthwise into strips about ¼ inch thick, separating any
leaves that are still attached together. Add to the bowl
along with the dates, 6 tablespoons of the pistachios, and
the capers. Toss well and season to taste with salt and
pepper. Sprinkle the reserved nuts on top and serve.

Choose-Your-Style Kale Salad

—

SERVES 4

1 pound kale

About 3 tablespoons extra-virgin olive oil, depending on the stiffness of your kale

1 teaspoon kosher salt, or more to taste, depending on the saltiness of the cheese you use

Everyone's favorite superfood combined with a salty cheese of your choice is as healthy as it is addictive. Don't forget to massage the kale!

START HERE

1. Cut the thick stems off the kale and reserve for pickling (see Note, page 114). Strip the leaves off the stems by pulling them away from the bottom up, and tear them into bite-size pieces. Rinse and blot dry.

2. Put the leaves in a large bowl, sprinkle with the olive oil and salt, and, using your hands, knead the oil and salt into the leaves for about a minute, until they glisten uniformly, to tenderize the kale. Choose your style (opposite), or pick one item from each row. Add your choice of flavorings, check the seasoning, and serve.

NOW YOU KNOW

Pickling Red Onions

There's hardly a salad, sandwich, plate of eggs, cheese and charcuterie board, or platter of meat that wouldn't be happier joined by a heap of pickled red onions. Here's how to make them: Slice an onion ⅛ inch thick and place in a small heatproof bowl. Combine 1 cup white wine vinegar, 1 cup sugar, and a pinch of kosher salt in a small saucepan and bring to a boil over medium heat. Boil gently, stirring occasionally, for a minute or two, until the sugar is completely dissolved. Pour over the onions and let steep until cool. Use right away or store refrigerated in the brine in a tightly covered container for up to 2 weeks.

CHOOSE YOUR STYLE

BLUE CHEESE	SMOKED CHEDDAR	GRANA PADANO	RICOTTA SALATA

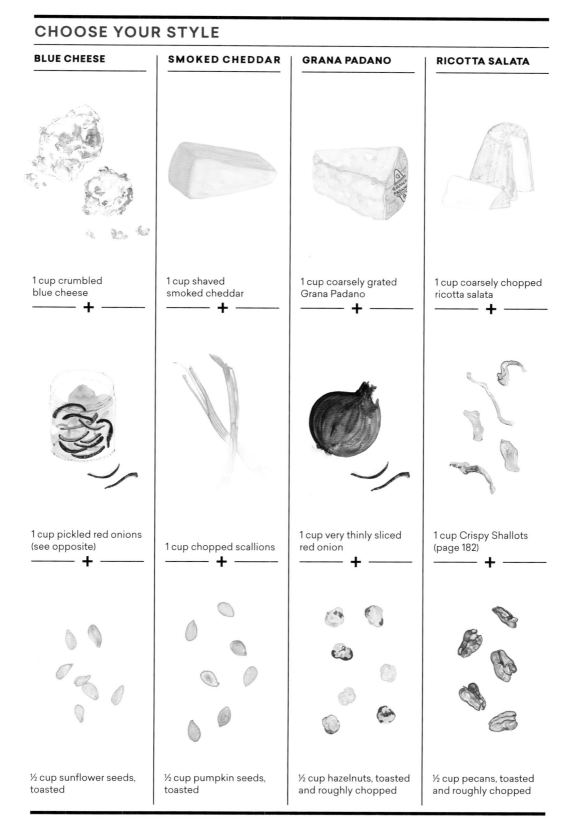

1 cup crumbled blue cheese	1 cup shaved smoked cheddar	1 cup coarsely grated Grana Padano	1 cup coarsely chopped ricotta salata
+	+	+	+
1 cup pickled red onions (see opposite)	1 cup chopped scallions	1 cup very thinly sliced red onion	1 cup Crispy Shallots (page 182)
+	+	+	+
½ cup sunflower seeds, toasted	½ cup pumpkin seeds, toasted	½ cup hazelnuts, toasted and roughly chopped	½ cup pecans, toasted and roughly chopped

Caramelized Endives and Gem Lettuces with Sheep's-Milk Cheese and Black Olives

—

SERVES 4

2 endives and 2 gem lettuces, rough outer leaves removed, or 4 large endives (about 4 ounces each)

3 tablespoons extra-virgin olive oil, plus more for drizzling

Kosher salt and freshly ground black pepper

6 ounces plain yogurt (sheep's-milk yogurt if available)

4 ounces sheep's-milk cheese, such as Istara or young Pecorino

8 pitted kalamata olives, torn lengthwise into rough pieces

1 cup Garlic Croutons (recipe follows), chopped into coarse crumbs

¾ cup loosely packed flat-leaf parsley

Silky, sweet, salty, crunchy—this has it all. And in the dead of winter, we all welcome a dish with ingredients that can be found in the cupboard and the corner store.

1. Preheat the oven to 425°F.

2. Slice the endives and lettuces lengthwise in half and trim the bottoms, leaving enough of the cores to hold the leaves together. Toss with the olive oil and arrange cut side down on a sheet pan. Sprinkle with salt and pepper and roast for about 15 minutes, until nicely browned on the bottom. Flip the endives and lettuces with a spatula and baste with additional olive oil if they seem dry. Roast for about 7 more minutes, until tender when pierced with a fork. Remove from the oven.

3. Spoon a large dollop of yogurt onto each individual serving plate or spoon the yogurt onto a platter, spreading it out with the back of the spoon. Arrange the endive and lettuces cut side up over it and shave slices of the cheese over the top (see Quick Cut, page 85). Shower with the olives, crouton crumbs, and parsley. Drizzle with a bit more olive oil, sprinkle with salt and pepper, and serve.

Continued

GARLIC CROUTONS

—

MAKES ABOUT 1 CUP

Garlic Oil

3 tablespoons extra-virgin olive oil

1 large garlic clove

A 3-ounce piece of good country or sourdough bread

1. Make the garlic oil: Pour the olive oil into a small bowl. Using a Microplane, grate the garlic into the oil, then stir it around to infuse the oil. Strain.

3. Cut the bread into ½-inch cubes, spread them out in a skillet, and drizzle with the garlic oil. Set over medium-high heat and toast, tossing occasionally, for 4 to 5 minutes, or until golden brown and crisp. Drain on paper towels. Store in an airtight container for up to a week.

MORE USES FOR GARLIC OIL |

- In place of unflavored oil in salad dressings

- Drizzled over vegetables before roasting and serving over hot pasta with grated Parmesan

- In place of butter for scrambled eggs

Black-Eyed Peas with Blood Oranges and Chipotle

SERVES 6 TO 8

1 pound dried black-eyed peas, picked over and rinsed

Kosher salt

3 blood oranges or 2 large navel oranges, zested and suprêmed (see Quick Cut, page 181), 1 tablespoon zest and ¼ cup juice reserved, segments broken into 3 or 4 pieces

Orange Chipotle Dressing

1 or 2 canned chipotle chiles in adobo sauce, plus 1½ teaspoons of the sauce, or more if desired

1½ teaspoons seasoned rice vinegar

1½ teaspoons Dijon mustard

½ cup flavorless vegetable oil

Kosher salt and freshly ground black pepper

½ cup chopped red onion

A good handful of fresh cilantro sprigs, or to taste

Freshly ground black pepper

The perfect balance of earthy, fruity, and spicy, this is an unusual twist on the traditional southern dish for prosperity in the New Year.

1. Bring the peas to a boil in a large pot of water. Reduce the heat and cook until they are tender but not mushy, anywhere from 30 minutes to 1 hour, depending on their age. Salt the water toward the end of the cooking time. Test for doneness by tasting several beans from different parts of the pot. Drain thoroughly and transfer to a large bowl.

2. While the peas are cooking, make the dressing: Combine the orange zest and juice, chiles, adobo sauce, vinegar, and mustard in the bowl of a food processor or in a blender and pulse to mix. With the motor running, slowly add the oil, processing until the dressing is smooth. Season to taste with salt and pepper.

3. Add the red onion, orange segments, dressing, and most of the cilantro to the bowl with the black-eyed peas and toss well. Season to taste with salt and pepper and add more adobo sauce if desired. Scatter the remaining cilantro over the top and serve.

Continued

Suprêming Citrus Fruit

For pieces of pure fruit, without any membrane or pith:

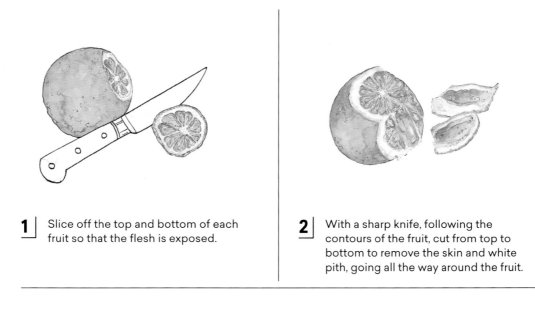

1 | Slice off the top and bottom of each fruit so that the flesh is exposed.

2 | With a sharp knife, following the contours of the fruit, cut from top to bottom to remove the skin and white pith, going all the way around the fruit.

3 | Holding the fruit over a bowl, cut along the membranes on both sides of each segment, allowing the segments to drop into the bowl.

Korean Rice Cakes with Kimchi Dressing and Crispy Shallots

—

SERVES 6 TO 8

Kosher salt

Kimchi Dressing

⅓ cup chopped drained kimchi, liquid reserved

1 teaspoon Dijon mustard

⅓ cup flavorless vegetable oil

1 tablespoon gochujang, or to taste (see page 17)

One 1-pound bag frozen disk-shaped Korean rice cakes, defrosted

3½ cups thinly sliced Napa cabbage (about 12 ounces)

½ cup chopped drained kimchi

2 tablespoons chopped fresh garlic chives or regular chives

Freshly ground black pepper

Crispy Shallots

8 ounces shallots (6 or 7 large), thinly sliced lengthwise

1 cup flavorless vegetable oil

Kosher salt

Cabbage with lots of garlic, in different guises. The crispy shallots are chef David Tanis's trick: Start them in room-temperature oil and cook them slowly to get them crisp without burning.

1. Bring a large pot of salted water to a boil. Meanwhile, make the dressing: Combine the kimchi, 1 tablespoon of the reserved liquid, and the mustard in the bowl of a food processor or in a blender. With the motor running, drizzle in the oil, processing until the mixture is smooth. Blend in the gochujang. Set aside.

2. Add the rice cakes to the boiling water and cook for about 5 minutes, until pliable. They will still be somewhat chewy. Drain the rice cakes in a colander and run cold water over them briefly to cool, then drain and transfer to a bowl. Toss with a few tablespoons of the dressing to prevent sticking.

3. Add the cabbage, chopped kimchi, and garlic chives to the rice cakes and toss well with the remaining dressing. Season to taste with salt and pepper.

4. Make the crispy shallots: Put the shallots in a small saucepan and cover them with the oil. Set the pan over medium heat and cook gently, stirring occasionally, until the shallots gradually turn brown, about 15 minutes. Lift them out with a slotted spoon and spread out on paper towels to drain; they will crisp up as they cool. Season with salt to taste while still warm. Strain the oil and store in the refrigerator for sautéing greens, or to use in any dressing where you'd like an additional layer of flavor.

5. Toss the rice cakes with most of the crispy shallots, then scatter the rest over the top and serve.

Korean Rice Cakes

There'll be a trip to the Asian grocer for the Korean rice cakes, usually found frozen. They come in disk shapes or small logs. Their toothsome texture is addictive. You can use them as you would any short pasta and serve with an assertive sauce (try them with Spicy Thai Basil Pesto, page 98).

Acorn Squash with Green Olives and Curry Dressing

—

SERVES 4

1½ pounds acorn squash, halved lengthwise, seeds scooped out, and sliced about an inch thick

2 tablespoons flavorless vegetable oil

Kosher salt and freshly ground black pepper

Curry Dressing

1 teaspoon cumin seeds

½ teaspoon coriander seeds

½ teaspoon fennel seeds

4 green cardamom pods

½ teaspoon ground ginger

¼ teaspoon ground turmeric

¾ teaspoon Dijon mustard

2½ tablespoons cider vinegar

½ cup flavorless vegetable oil

Kosher salt and freshly ground black pepper

½ pound Savoy cabbage, cored and thinly sliced crosswise into ⅛-inch-wide ribbons

¼ cup pitted green olives, halved and thinly sliced

½ cup raisins or Pickled Raisins (page 144)

¼ cup sliced almonds, toasted

In this unusual take on a usual squash, the green olives and Indian flavors in the dressing spice up the caramelized acorn squash wedges.

1. Preheat the oven to 400°F.

2. On a sheet pan, toss the squash slices with the oil and season with salt and pepper to taste. Spread the slices out and roast for about 20 minutes, until tender and nicely browned in parts, turning once halfway through. Let cool.

3. While the squash is roasting, make the dressing: Toast the whole spices in a small skillet over medium heat for several minutes, stirring occasionally, until fragrant. Grind together in a mortar or spice grinder. Add the ginger and turmeric. Put the mustard and vinegar in the bowl of a food processor or in a blender, add the spices, and pulse to combine. Gradually add the oil, processing until the dressing is well blended. Season to taste with salt and pepper.

4. Combine the cabbage, olives, raisins, and almonds in a large bowl and toss with half of the curry dressing. Add the squash and toss gently with the remaining dressing, taking care not to break the squash slices. Adjust the seasoning with salt and pepper if necessary and serve.

Grapefruit Salad with Dates and Dried Cherries

—

SERVES 4

2 large pink or red grapefruits

¾ teaspoon Dijon mustard

¼ teaspoon honey, or more to taste

3 tablespoons extra-virgin olive oil

Kosher salt and freshly ground black pepper

3 large Medjool dates, pitted

¼ cup dried cherries

1 head of red leaf lettuce, separated into leaves, washed, and dried

2 tablespoons toasted sunflower seeds

Scant ½ teaspoon flaky salt

2 to 3 scallions, green parts only, thinly sliced on the diagonal

Jewel-toned and refreshing, this salad is a tart and sweet addition to a weekend brunch.

1. With a sharp knife, peel the grapefruits, carefully removing all the white pith. Slice off the tops and bottoms and slice the fruit into rounds ½ inch thick or thinner. Transfer to a bowl, along with any juices—squeeze the trimmings to get every last drop. (The grapefruit can be prepared a day ahead of time and refrigerated.)

2. Make the dressing: Pour 3 tablespoons of the grapefruit juice into a small bowl. Whisk in the mustard and honey. Slowly whisk in the olive oil. Season to taste with salt and pepper. Set aside.

3. Slice the dates lengthwise into quarters, then cut crosswise into small dice. Place in a small bowl. If the cherries are large, chop them. Add the cherries to the dates and stir in 1 tablespoon of the dressing to keep the fruit from sticking together.

4. Line a platter with the lettuce leaves. Arrange the slices of grapefruit on top of the lettuce and season with salt and pepper to taste. Scatter the dried fruit over the grapefruit and lettuce and drizzle with the remaining dressing. Shower with the sunflower seeds, flaky salt, and scallion greens and serve.

Jazzed-Up Potato Salad

—

SERVES 4

1½ pounds small new potatoes, cut in half, or quartered if large

Kosher salt

3 tablespoons extra-virgin olive oil, plus more for drizzling

Pickled Carrots (recipe follows), plus 3 tablespoons of the pickling liquid

Freshly ground black pepper

2 celery stalks, trimmed and sliced on the diagonal

2 scallions, sliced on the diagonal (about ⅓ cup)

⅓ cup kalamata olives, pitted and halved lengthwise

Briny black olives and tart pickled carrots add unexpected notes to this classic dish.

1. Place the potatoes in a large saucepan, cover with cold water by several inches, add salt to taste, and bring to a boil over high heat. Lower the heat to medium and cook for about 8 minutes, or until the potatoes can be pierced through with the sharp point of a knife. Drain in a colander. While the potatoes are still warm, add 2 tablespoons of the olive oil and 2 tablespoons of the pickling liquid from the carrots, and season to taste with salt and pepper. Let cool.

2. When the potatoes have cooled, add the drained pickled carrots, the celery, scallions, and remaining 1 tablespoon each olive oil and pickling liquid and toss gently, taking care not to break the potatoes. Add the olives, season to taste with salt and pepper, and toss again. Drizzle with additional olive oil and serve.

PICKLED CARROTS

—

MAKES ABOUT ⅓ CUP

1 medium carrot, peeled and grated

¼ cup sugar

¼ cup white wine vinegar

A pinch of kosher salt

1. Put the carrot in a small heatproof bowl. Combine the sugar, vinegar, and salt in a small saucepan and bring to a boil over medium heat. Boil gently, stirring occasionally, for a minute or two, until the sugar is completely dissolved. Pour over the carrot and steep until cool. Use right away or store refrigerated in the brine in a tightly covered container for up to 2 weeks.

2. Drain the carrot before using, but reserve the liquid.

A Cold-Weather Comfort Menu

When the wind is howling, gather your closest friends for a cozy dinner. Enjoy the meal by a crackling fire. Double, triple, or quadruple recipes as necessary to feed your crowd.

—

MAKE THIS:

Sourdough Bread Salad (page 116)

Broccoli Rabe with Roasted Oyster Mushrooms (page 163)

ADD THIS:

Alpine Cheese Board (opposite)

Herb-and-Lemon-Brined Roast Chicken (opposite)

BUY THIS:

Apple or pear cider

Hot chocolate and marshmallows

Alpine Cheese Board

—

Alpine cheeses, produced high in the mountains, are nutty and fruity, tasting of the grass the cows graze on. It's fun to compare and contrast a variety of them, so select at least three (such as Gruyère, Comté, raclette, Tomme de Savoie, Reblochon, and/or Fontina Val d'Aosta).

Along with the cheeses, offer guests hot (spicy) honey, such as Mike's, and apple butter, such as Kime's or Eden. Serve with small plates and sharp knives, a bowl of small, pretty apples, and a sliced baguette or bread of your choosing.

Herb-and-Lemon-Brined Roast Chicken

—

MAKES 1 CHICKEN

Combine 1½ quarts water, ¾ cup kosher salt, 3 tablespoons honey or sugar, 8 bay leaves, 1 large or 2 small halved heads of garlic, 3 fresh sprigs rosemary, 1 small bunch of thyme, 1 small bunch of flat-leaf parsley, and 3 lemon halves in a large stockpot and bring to a boil. Remove from the heat and let cool. Stir in 1½ additional quarts cold water. Make sure the brine is completely cool before you add the chicken.

Submerge a 3½-pound chicken in the brine, breast side down, and refrigerate for 1 to 2 days. Half an hour before you are ready to roast, drain the chicken. Pat the bird very dry with paper towels. Tuck the wings under, tie the legs together with butcher's twine, and set on a rack in a shallow roasting pan or on a sheet pan. Let come to room temperature while you preheat the oven to 425°F.

Roast the chicken for about 50 minutes, rotating the pan halfway through, until an instant-read thermometer placed in the thickest part of one of the thighs reads 165°F. Transfer the chicken to a carving board and let rest for about 10 minutes before cutting away the twine and carving into serving pieces.

Appendix: Vegetarian, Vegan, and Gluten-Free Recipes

Recipe (subrecipes and variations are in *italics*)	Vegetarian	Vegan	Gluten-Free
Acorn Squash with Green Olives and Curry Dressing (page 185)	V	VV	GF
Alpine Cheese Board (page 193)	V		★
Baby Carrots with Carrot-Top Pesto (page 34)	V		GF
Barley with Many Mushrooms (page 149)	V	VV	
Beans and Sprouts, Bacon and Sorrel (page 138)			GF
Black-Eyed Peas with Blood Oranges and Chipotle (page 179)	V	VV	GF
Black Rice with Pea Greens (page 30)	V	VV	GF
Bosc Pear and Fennel Slaw (page 120)	V	★★	GF
Broccoli Rabe with Roasted Oyster Mushrooms (page 163)			GF
Cabbage and Kraut (page 167)	V	★★	GF
Cabbage and Kimchi (page 167)	★★★	★★ ★★★	GF
Caramelized Endives and Gem Lettuce with Sheep's-Milk Cheese and Black Olives (page 176)	V		
Garlic Croutons (page 178)	V	VV	
Charred Summer Squash with Spicy Cucumbers (page 81)	V	VV	GF
Chilled Soba and Smoked Salmon in Yuzu Kosho Broth (page 101)			★
Choose-Your-Style Brussels Sprouts			
Kasbah (page 147)	V	★★	GF
Mideast (page 147)	V	VV	GF
Tex-Mex (page 147)	V	VV	GF
Yankee (page 147)			GF
Choose-Your-Style Japanese Eggplant Boats			
Drizzled (page 77)	V		GF
Flecked (page 77)			GF
Laden (page 77)	V	VV	GF

★   If using gluten-free versions of the following products: tamari, oats, bread, Bhel mix
★★ Honey can be replaced with a vegan sweetener (sugar, agave, etc.)
★★★ If using vegetarian/vegan kimchi (such as Mother-in-Law's brand)

Recipe (subrecipes and variations are in *italics*)	Vegetarian	Vegan	Gluten-Free
Striped (page 77)	V	VV	GF
Choose-Your-Style Kale Salad			
Blue Cheese (page 175)	V		GF
Grana Padano (page 175)	V		GF
Ricotta Salata (page 175)	V		GF
Smoked Cheddar (page 175)	V		GF
Choose-Your-Style Tiny Tomatoes			
(Almost) BLT-Style (page 69)			
At the Taverna (page 69)	V		GF
Sweet & Nutty (page 69)	V	VV	GF
Vivid & Surprising (page 69)	V	VV	GF
Cold-Weather Crudités with Seeded Yogurt Dip (page 158)	V		GF
Corn × 3 (page 89)	V	VV	GF
Couscous and Spring Allium Mix (page 25)	V	VV	
Watercress Dressing (page 26)	V	VV	GF
Cucumbers with Black Sesame Seeds and Sweet Lime Vinegar (page 92)	V	VV	GF
Sweet Lime Vinegar (page 92)	V	VV	GF
Dried Fruit Compote (page 155)	V	VV	GF
Every-Leafy-Green-You-Can-Find Salad (page 37)	V	VV	GF
Farro with Five Jewels (page 143)	V	VV	
Pickled Raisins (page 144)	V	VV	GF
Gem Lettuces, Avocado, and Tomatillo with Buttermilk Dressing (page 107)	V		GF
Tomatillo Salsa (page 108)	V	VV	GF
Grapefruit Salad with Dates and Dried Cherries (page 189)	V	**	GF
Gruyère and Avocado Sandwiches (page 103)	V		
Hard-Boiled Eggs with Green Olive Mayonnaise (page 61)	V		GF
Herb-and-Lemon-Brined Roast Chicken (page 193)			GF
"Horse and Pig" Sandwiches (page 103)			
I Heart Fennel (page 119)	V	VV	GF
It's All Green (page 54)	V	VV	GF
Avocado Mint Dip (page 56)	V	VV	GF

   *   If using gluten-free versions of the following products: tamari, oats, bread, Bhel mix

  ** Honey can be replaced with a vegan sweetener (sugar, agave, etc.)

*** If using vegetarian/vegan kimchi (such as Mother-in-Law's brand)

Recipe (subrecipes and variations are in *italics*)	Vegetarian	Vegan	Gluten-Free
Cilantro Cumin Dip (page 56)	V	VV	GF
Cucumber Shallot Dip (page 55)			GF
Pumpkin Seed Hummus (page 55)	V	VV	GF
Sweet Lime Salt (page 57)	V	VV	GF
Jazzed-Up Potato Salad (page 190)	V	VV	GF
Pickled Carrots (page 190)	V	VV	GF
Korean Rice Cakes with Kimchi Dressing and Crispy Shallots (page 182)	***	***	GF
Maple-Miso Butternut Squash (page 123)	V	VV	GF
Maple-Miso Dressing (page 123)	V	VV	GF
New Potatoes with Soft Green Herbs (page 53)	V		GF
Not-Exactly-Manchurian Cauliflower (page 129)	V	VV	GF
Palest Green (page 124)	V	VV	GF
"Peas and Carrots" on Papadum (page 33)	V	**	GF
Coriander Dressing (page 33)	V	**	GF
Pink Peppered Potato Vodka Shots with Petals (page 155)	V	VV	GF
Potatoes and Cucumbers with Caraway and All Kinds of Mustard (page 87)	V	**	GF
Pickled Mustard Seeds (page 88)	V	VV	GF
Really Yellow (page 71)	V		*
Six-Minute Eggs (page 72)	V		GF
Red (page 113)	V	**	GF
Red Cabbage and Chickpeas with a Kick (page 168)	V	VV	GF
Spicy Tahini Dressing (page 169)	V	VV	GF
Red Potatoes with Chorizo and Roasted Grapes (page 151)			GF
Roasted Grapes (page 152)	V	VV	GF
Rice Noodles with Lots of Asian Herbs (page 38)	V	VV	GF
Lime Dressing (page 38)	V	VV	GF
Roasted and Pickled Cauliflower (page 126)	V		GF
Roots and Leaves (page 135)	V	VV	GF
Savory Granola (page 61)	V	VV	*
Semi-Scorched Chive Buds with Smoked Tofu (page 40)	V	VV	*
Silky Tofu Skin with Preserved Cabbage Dressing (page 43)	V		GF

* If using gluten-free versions of the following products: tamari, oats, bread, Bhel mix

** Honey can be replaced with a vegan sweetener (sugar, agave, etc.)

*** If using vegetarian/vegan kimchi (such as Mother-in-Law's brand)

Recipe (subrecipes and variations are in *italics*)	Vegetarian	Vegan	Gluten-Free
Slightly Spicy Carrots with Buckwheat Honey (page 161)	V		GF
Smoked Trout and Pumpernickel Bread Salad (page 49)			
Smoky, Spicy Okra and Cherry Tomatoes (page 66)	V	VV	GF
Snap Peas and Other Things Spring (page 29)	V	VV	GF
Sourdough Bread Salad (page 116)	V		
Sunchoke and Endive Slaw (page 173)	V	VV	GF
Sweet Potatoes and Chickpeas, Bhel Puri Style (page 141)	V	VV	★
Fresh Green Chutney (page 142)	V	VV	GF
Tabouleh-esque (page 95)	V	VV	
Tex-Mex Cornbread Salad (page 73)	V		
Three-Bean Salad (Kinda) (page 96)	V	VV	GF
Toasty Broccoli with Curry Leaves and Coconut (page 131)	V	VV	GF
Tofu Shirataki Noodles with Spicy Thai Basil Pesto (page 98)			GF
Tomato Wedges, Lemon Onions, and Bok Choy (page 65)	V	VV	GF
Vietnamese-Style Tofu Salad (page 47)	V	★★	★
Carrot-Daikon Pickle (page 48)	V	VV	GF
Watermelon with Chrysanthemum and Shiso (page 79)	V		GF
Yellow Beets and Harissa Onions (page 109)	V	VV	GF
Zucchini Ribbons with Squash Blossoms (page 85)	V		GF

★   If using gluten-free versions of the following products: tamari, oats, bread, Bhel mix

★★   Honey can be replaced with a vegan sweetener (sugar, agave, etc.)

★★★   If using vegetarian/vegan kimchi (such as Mother-in-Law's brand)

Sources

My shop, R&D Foods, carries all of my favorite condiments as well as a selection of the more unusual spices and dry goods called for in these recipes. Find them at our online store (rdfoodsbklyn.com/pantry), or, if you are in the neighborhood, please stop by (602 Vanderbilt Avenue, Brooklyn, New York). Other recommended purveyors:

Crazy Korean Cooking
crazykoreancooking.com
Gochujang, gochugaru, rice cakes, and other Korean specialties

Despaña
New York, NY
despanabrandfoods.com
Pimenton de la Vera, Spanish chorizo, other Spanish specialties

Fresh Bites Basket
freshbitesbasket.com
Black rice, rice noodles, yuzu kosho, tofu skin, soba, dried shrimp, and a wide selection of other Asian ingredients

Heatonist
Brooklyn, NY
heatonist.com
Assorted hot sauces, harissa

Kalustyan's
New York, NY
kalustyans.com
Papadums, Bhel mix and other Indian snack mixes, goji berries, hominy, coconut chips, za'atar, harissas, nigella seeds, oreganos, gochugaru, tahini, curry leaves, makrut lime leaves, dried corn, and many more Indian and Middle Eastern specialties

Mother-in-Law's
milkimchi.com
Kimchi, gochujang, and other Korean products, including vegan options

Penzeys Spices
penzeys.com
General spices and blends

Pollen Ranch
pollenranch.com
Fennel pollen, spice blends

Savory Spice Shop
savoryspiceshop.com
General spices and blends

Seed & Mill
seedandmill.com
Tahini, halva, sesame spice blends

South River Miso
southrivermiso.com
Adzuki bean miso, white (shiro) miso

Acknowledgments

A giant heartfelt thank-you to . . .

All the smart and creative folks at Artisan: Lia Ronnen, Michelle Ishay-Cohen, Renata Di Biase, Erica Heitman-Ford, Sibylle Kazeroid, Judith Sutton, Nancy Murray, and Hanh Le; our editor extraordinaire, Bridget Monroe Itkin, for her dedication, patience, and grace; and especially Ann Bramson, for championing me in the first place.

My collaborator, Donna Gelb, for sticking it out for the long haul and always showing up with kindness, generosity, and all the recipes organized.

Joey De Leo for stunning photographs and special accommodations, and stylists Michelle Gatton for a perfect turn of leaf and drip of oil and Micah Morton for the eleventh-hour elegance. Sarah Jackson for all the perfect behind-the-scenes photo session prep. Emma Dibben for her charming illustrations.

Barbara and Alberto Gatenio for many things great and small over so many decades (photo set included!).

Sara Dima, my friend and business partner, for showing up day after day, year after year—no small accomplishment.

Maury Rubin for giving me a platform, for years of encouragement, and for teaching me, among other things, to embrace my "stickler gene."

All the farmers, artisans, and makers whose products never cease to inspire me.

All my staff members, past and present, for their hard work and fortitude.

My husband, Mark, for being an unwavering cheerleader.

And my daughters, Hannah and Isabel, for whom there are no words. . . .

—

Donna Gelb would also like to thank Ann Bramson for her vision, trust, and support; Lia Ronnen for her wisdom; the heroic Bridget Monroe Itkin for pulling it all together; and the rest of the amazing Artisan team. In addition, thank you to Ilene Rosen for the journey, the lessons, and especially the laughs. Thanks to my sons, David and Matthew, for their constant encouragement and humor, and to Joanne Edelstein and Marta Matos for their sharp recipe testing help and super-discerning palates.

Index

Conversion Charts

Here are rounded-off equivalents between the metric system and the traditional systems that are used in the United States to measure weight and volume.

Weights

US/UK	Metric
1 oz	30 g
2 oz	55 g
3 oz	85 g
4 oz (¼ lb)	115 g
5 oz	140 g
6 oz	170 g
7 oz	200 g
8 oz (½ lb)	225 g
9 oz	255 g
10 oz	285 g
11 oz	310 g
12 oz	340 g
13 oz	370 g
14 oz	395 g
15 oz	425 g
16 oz (1 lb)	455 g

Volume

American	Imperial	Metric
¼ tsp		1.25 ml
½ tsp		2.5 ml
1 tsp		5 ml
½ Tbsp (1½ tsp)		7.5 ml
1 Tbsp (3 tsp)		15 ml
¼ cup (4 Tbsp)	2 fl oz	60 ml
⅓ cup (5 Tbsp)	2½ fl oz	75 ml
½ cup (8 Tbsp)	4 fl oz	125 ml
⅔ cup (10 Tbsp)	5 fl oz	150 ml
¾ cup (12 Tbsp)	6 fl oz	175 ml
1 cup (16 Tbsp)	8 fl oz	250 ml
1¼ cups	10 fl oz	300 ml
1½ cups	12 fl oz	350 ml
2 cups (1 pint)	16 fl oz	500 ml
2½ cups	20 fl oz (1 pint)	625 ml
5 cups	40 fl oz (1 qt)	1.25 ml

Oven Temperatures

	°F	°C	Gas Mark
very cool	250–275	130–140	½–1
cool	300	148	2
warm	325	163	3
moderate	350	177	4
moderately hot	375–400	190–204	5–6
hot	425	218	7
very hot	450–475	232–245	8–9